GHOSTS OF JEFFERSON BARRACKS

History & Hauntings of Old St. Louis

BY DAVID GOODWIN

~ A Whitechapel Productions Press Publication ~

Original Cover Artwork Designed by
Michael Schwab, M & S Graphics & Troy Taylor
Visit M & S Graphics at www.msgrfx.com

This Book is Published by
~ Whitechapel Productions Press ~
A Division of the History & Hauntings Book Co.
515 East Third Street ~ Alton, Illinois ~62002
(618) 465~1086 / 1~888~GHOSTLY
Visit us on the Internet at www.prairieghosts.com

First Printing ~ December 2001
ISBN: 1~892523~19~1

Printed in the United States of America

Far better it is to dare mighty things, to win glorious triumphs, even though checkered by failure, than to take rank with those poor spirits who neither enjoy nor suffer too much, because they live in the gray twilight that knows not victory nor defeat.

THEODORE ROOSEVELT

I must emphasize that one can only be one's own guinea pig in the matters of the supernatural. No spoken or written word can be a substitute for one's own practical experience. No one too can convince another who does not wish to believe what he or she is told. Only the doubter loses by his or her incredulity.

T.C. LETHBRIDGE - "GHOST AND GHOUL"

Eternal vigilance is the price of liberty

THOMAS JEFFERSON

Wherever the soldiers of our little army are marshalled, whether on tented field, in frowning fortress, or on embattled plain- wherever the rainbow- striped and star-jeweled flag of our country waves over company or battalion, there will be found brave hearts and generous spirits, that will throb and glow with grateful emotions, at the memory of Jefferson Barracks, their gallant commander, and his accomplished family

J.C. WILD, 1841

Rest my dear, I will be here,
Even though you need me not,
And never will I ever fear
What haunts this deathly spot.

H.P. LOVECRAFT

Memorial to the Unknown Dead, 1861-1865
On fame's eternal camping ground
Their silent tents are spread
While glory guards with solemn sound
The bivouac of the dead

ANNIE WHITTENMEYER

INTRODUCTION

I have had three true infatuations in my life that did not involve a member of the opposite sex. My first passion developed when I was 12 years old. I remember that summer vacation in 1979 as if it were yesterday. That summer, my father took our family to Fort Michilimackinac for vacation. From the minute I set my eyes on this colonial stockade, located at the northern tip of Michigan's Lower Peninsula, I was forever enamored with forts and their requisite influence throughout history. This trip would also springboard me into a fascination with libraries and reading that has been invaluable to me through the years.

During my formative junior high and high school years, I stumbled across my second true passion. As a result of my exposure to libraries, and because of my unexplainable interest in occult subjects, I became an ardent student of ghosts and other mysterious supernatural phenomena. The library in my hometown of Marquette Michigan did not have a huge selection of books on the topic of ghosts, UFO's and monsters, but it was a guarantee that if they had a tome available on one of these subjects, I had read it at least twice. Later, I would help to create the now defunct Marquette Center for Paranormal Research (M.C.P.R.) and I became a member of the Ghost Research Society. Today, I am actively involved in the American Ghost Society as an Area Representative for Missouri and I am still active in the Ghost Research Society, serving as the State Coordinator for Missouri as well.

As a result of my enlistment in the Michigan Army National Guard in 1986 and my later involvement in the Reserve Officer Training Corps (ROTC) at Northern Michigan University, I became engrossed in my third area of interest, military history. My continued military training and assignments as a young second lieutenant would require that I be well versed about historic battles, great generals, and sometimes, about great military blunders. I found each topic exhilarating and even found that some of the information presented was useful in regards to leading soldiers in the 21st century.

All three of my passions ran headlong into each other when, in November 1998, I was assigned to Jefferson Barracks as the Battalion Logistics Officer (S4) for the 1138th Engineer Battalion. The first time I visited Jefferson Barracks, I actually felt like I was entering a fold in time. I was in awe at the excellent condition of the historic buildings on post and I became intrigued by the stories that surrounded each of them. Shortly after I became Detachment Commander of my unit in 1999, my soldiers started telling me about the ghosts.....

This book is a culmination of my obsessions. My goal in compiling this collection of stories was to capture the varied and unnerving paranormal experiences of the professional soldiers stationed at Jefferson Barracks through the years while at the same time imparting a little historical information along the way.

I personally know many of the soldiers mentioned in the following pages. These men and women have received various levels of military training and are not prone to "flights of fancy". They are by virtue of their profession very serious folk. In some instances, many of these same soldiers have fought in foreign lands, in defense of their country.

When I first started soliciting for stories, I initially thought that many soldiers, including my own, and many civilian employees working at Jefferson Barracks would look at me and just shake their heads in disbelief that I was even considering writing a book about ghosts. In reality, I got the exact opposite reaction. Soldiers of all ranks and civilians at all levels seemed eager to share their ghostly encounters with me. In some instances soldiers would tell me “my story is not that interesting” or “I never really saw anything but I heard....”. In most cases like these, by the time my interview with them was concluded, they realized that they had more of a story to share with me than they thought.

In some instances, I have not included the names of the soldiers or employees involved in a particular encounter. This was done at the request of the interviewee or if the person just seemed very hesitant about letting me identify them in relation to the particular story being told. If there has been one common thread that has linked each of the interviews that I have done, it would be that each personal ghostly encounter that has been told to me, has been related to me with stalwart conviction and compassion.

The remainder of the book is, in itself, a history lesson. I have made every attempt to ensure that the historical information contained in the following pages, is as accurate as possible.

David L. Goodwin
August 2001

CHAPTER ONE

MILITARY FORTIFICATIONS 101

Our food is abominable; when you break a biscuit, you can see it move (if the critters are not dead from eating bad flour).The pork and bacon are of the same character. We would not mind this so much if they would only serve us out enough.... If not for wild beef we shoot, we should starve.

AN AMERICAN SOLDIER, WRITING HOME IN 1846 CAMP BILKNAP, TEXAS

Before you can truly begin to appreciate Jefferson Barracks's intriguing history and then later be able to explore the varied incidents of paranormal activity that seem to be in abundance there, you must first understand the basic theory behind the importance of military fortifications. This chapter is a very brief introduction to military engineering, and its critical role in the development of fortifications throughout history. As you have probably already figured out, you will not be able to get college credit for reading this over-view. It serves primarily as a starting point for our examination of the "Ghosts of Jefferson Barracks".

EARLY FORTIFICATIONS

Since time immemorial, humans have always had a knack for banding together into small groups. During pre-historic times, this was done for the safety and survival of the clan. As time passed, these family groups, permanently settled in areas that were strategically located near plentiful natural resources, thus creating small hamlets of humanity that would eventually become villages and towns. Unfortunately, when you build something that is prosperous, some one who may not be as well off as you are will want to take it away from you. This harsh fact of life in the early development of civilization as we know it created the need to build fortifications.

In the 9th and 10th Centuries, the first fortifications were circles, squares, and rectangles made up of piled earth, rocks, and other natural debris. Many of these early earthworks were erected around residential areas, ceremonial courts, and even burial grounds. The primary goal of these early defenses was for protection against raids by nomads such as Vikings and Magyars (Hungarian nomads). Time would pass and these earthen and fort-like enclosures would be built on isolated hills at the center of the settlements to provide a home for the noble lord of the region. During times of war, these citadels would serve as a place of safety during times of attack. These early fortifications differed from later man made enclosures as they were designed to "fight from" and repel attackers. Early primitive stockades would develop over time into the motte-and-bailey castles that became common place during the Middle Ages.

It was during the 10th century that castles would begin to be built out of stone. Between the 11th and 15th centuries, the stone mid evil castle would dominate much of Europe. Early in the 14th century castles would start to see their decline with the advent of gunpowder making its appearance in Europe.

The bombard, or early cannon, and the overall stability of society at the time signaled the end of the European castle. By the 16th century, the prominence of the castle was all but in decline except in buffer zones or danger areas where they were used as a first line of defense against the Turks.

EARLY INDIAN EARTHWORKS IN THE CONTINENTAL UNITED STATES

French, Spanish, and English explorers, mapping the Mississippi Valley in the 16th, 17th, and 18th centuries would find evidence of far older earthworks and fortifications that had been built between 500 B.C. and A.D. 700.

These sometimes large and diverse mounds came in all different shapes and sizes. Today, platform, temple, burial and effigy mounds can be found in over 32 states. Though the creators of these mounds were a mystery to the early explorers and colonists who found them, archeological records have proven that the Adena, Hopewell, and the Mississippian native peoples built these massive earth structures.

It is unclear exactly what these earth and stone complexes were used for, but it is believed that some may have been used as actual fortifications, while others may have served as cultural or religious centers. Cahokia, located in Illinois, near St. Louis, is one of the largest Mississippian culture mound sites in existence.

EARLY COLONIAL FORTS IN AMERICA

When the first explorers and colonists arrived in North America in the 1500's, they built crude wooden forts for protection against the perceived threat of hostile Indians and the natural elements they faced. These wooden strongholds, usually made up of a stockade or blockhouse and a cannon or two, would serve as a cultural center, governmental center and as a religious base for inhabitants and the settlers living in the surrounding area. Later, these military posts would become booming economic centers for the fur trade and re-supply points for explorers charting the interior of the continent.

In theory, military engineers preferred to build defenses out of stone or other similar substances. In reality, the quantity, quality, and experience level of the construction crew on hand generally dictated what was used to build these fortifications. Forts built in the north were generally made of wood due to the abundance of virgin timber. Posts built in aired locations such as in the desert were made of adobe, a kind of clay and mud mixed together. Stone strongholds were constructed when the raw stone material, trained masons, and carpenters were available to do so.

In most instances, the same soldiers who would later garrison these posts were required to build them. This extremely "manual labor" caused some understandable bitterness in these would be Indian fighters. By the 1800's, the role of the fort would change significantly.

THE INFLUENCE OF THE LOUISIANA PURCHASE ON WESTERN FORTIFICATIONS

Forts on the frontier would not be places where soldiers would stand and fight, instead, they would become supply bases and depots used by military units as they patrolled the untamed West.

In 1803, President Thomas Jefferson's excellent negotiation skills brought about the settlement of the Louisiana Purchase. This now meant that military posts, garrisoned by American troops, became the primary means for a young United States to project its military might and influence into the vastness of the new republic. Posts along the western frontier such as Fort Bellefountaine, built in 1805 near the confluence of the Mississippi and Missouri Rivers, and Jefferson Barracks, established in 1826 south of St. Louis, would serve as beacons of light and hope to brave pioneers. More importantly, Fort Bellefountaine, Jefferson Barracks, and the numerous other fortifications built from the Mississippi River to the coast of California would insure America's claim to the vast new territories of the west. Ultimately, many of these desolate out of the way military encampments would be potent tools in the perpetuation of the common, if not misguided, American belief in the God given right of "Manifest Destiny".

CHAPTER TWO

THE ENIGMA OF HAUNTED MILITARY POSTS

Forts... as kids, we used to make them out of blankets in our bedrooms. When we were older, we constructed these hide-a-ways out of scrap lumber in the woods behind the house. No matter what you call them: depots, cantonments, presidios, forts or barracks, military posts have always captured the imaginations of both the young and old. The very word "fort" by itself, conjures up images of mystery, romance, intrigue, and grandeur. When you visit the few pioneer posts that are still existence today, one cannot help but imagine vivid images of gallant young soldiers vigilantly walking guard mount, or ranks of men in showy parade dress uniforms, completing rifle drill under the watchful eye of their company officers.

All too often, however, these old safe havens harbor more than the recognizable gift shop or display cannon. As you will soon see, the remnants of the past can still be present in old buildings and forts. Some times, what lies hidden behind the faded stockade wall or inside the hewn stone blockhouse, is something that can only be described as "supernatural".

ORIGINS AND THEORIES

No one really knows what ghosts are. To add to the mystery, no one can really quantify the reasons why a particular location, especially military posts, become haunted.

If you have ever read any literature about this esoteric topic or watched any cable television, you know that theories abound in the public realm when it comes to these questions. Unfortunately, many of the conclusions presented in the main stream media have no basis in scientific fact. They tend to be the babblings of some self-proclaimed expert in the paranormal field that generally wants you to buy his or her new book, or just wants you to "tune in next week". I argue however, that it is not possible for just one hypothesis to be able to account for all of the varied phenomena associated with each type of paranormal experience. I am supportive of the idea that several different factors when combined under the right circumstances can increase the likelihood that a given location will become haunted. In the remainder of this chapter, I will attempt to present some theories that I believe are the most plausibly accurate in regards to question of the origin of ghosts. They are an amalgamation of several different theories from numerous sources. I will further build on some of these ideas using several examples from different paranormal incidents that have been reported at other forts and military posts over the years.

By far the most common supernatural encounter reported by many soldiers stationed at Jefferson Barracks and other posts are that of unexplained noises or physical sensations. This type of ghostly encounter has been referred to as a "Residual" haunting.

People who experience this type of haunting report such things as mysterious tapping and knocking sounds, doors opening and closing by themselves, the turning on and off of electrical equipment and lights, and even ghostly footstep or muted voices. Also generally associated with a residual haunting, is the feeling of being watched, sudden (noticeable) temperature fluctuations, strange odors and the feeling of "goose bumps" on the surface of ones skin. In residual hauntings, apparitions are sometimes observed but they do not interact with the person who sees them.

The manifestation at the Military Intelligence School, Fort Devens, Massachusetts, is a good example of a residual haunting. The ghost that haunts Hale Hall, likes to slam doors, turn lights on and off, and is known to make the most retched noises. In most cases, what generally "creeps" out the person who experiences this type of haunting is the fact that upon further investigation, the origin of these phenomena will have no apparent, logical explanation.

It is possible that in many cases, the raw natural materials used in the construction of military posts have a direct correlation to the amount of "residual" spirit activity experienced at these locations throughout the years. Dense stone, exotic lumber, drainage, ventilation and varied (experimental) building techniques combine to create a template or membrane that is easily saturated by spirit energy. These very durable substances later serve as a battery, that every now and then releases the psychic energy we commonly refer to as ghostly phenomena. But as you know, even batteries loose their charge. There is some evidence to suggest that this type of haunting will wear down, become less active or pronounced, and even fade away forever over time. This may explain why so many castles in Europe are reportedly haunted.

The second, less frequent, type of ghost encountered at forts and military posts is considered "intelligent" or "interactive". This type of haunting is significant because the spirit of the deceased person actually interacts in an intelligent manner with the living observer. The "intelligent" spirit is the kind of ghost most frequently portrayed on TV and in movies. This type of paranormal manifestation is what people typically think of when they think of ghosts or the supernatural. This particular apparition is even more astounding because it haunts a location because it wants to be there. It is not dependant solely on location or types of building materials, though these factors could possibly influence the over all "power" this spirit possesses during manifestations. What most people do not realize is that the "intelligent" haunting can also produce many of the same physical characteristics as the residual haunting. Because of this, people sometimes get the two confused.

The ghost of Fort Bridger Cemetery, Wyoming, is a good example of an intelligent haunting. The caretaker of the cemetery reported that the ghost of an elderly man wearing a cowboy hat followed him around the grounds, and on several occasions appeared to have helped him in his chores. The ghost reportedly vanished around the time his wife passed away. The spirits actions and desire to be near his mate are classic examples of an intelligent haunting.

I would offer that the main reason that an interactive "psychic" spirit haunts a location, such as a military post, is because some traumatic event or series of events took place there over the years. Murder, suicide, untimely death due to disease, accident or misfortune can cause a person's spirit to resist passing on to the other side and force them to be embossed into the very natural fabric of a historic location. Sometimes, a person's spirit stays behind on purpose because of a misguided emotional attachment, good or bad, to a particular person, place or thing. In those rare instances, it is even possible that the spirit does not even know that he or she is no longer in the world of the living. If any one of these theories holds true, then an older location, such as is the case with Jefferson Barracks, will have a greater likelihood of being imprinted with extensive emotional events of this magnitude.

The following ghostly tales were selected because they had several things in common. First and most important, these locations are considered historic and of course they are allegedly haunted. Each has a colorful lineage predating the 1900's. These installations also share familiar stories of untimely death and other misfortunes. These stories are unique because several often reflect the cultural biases of past generations.

FORT PULASKI, GEORGIA

Savannah, Georgia is the home of the Fort Pulaski National monument. Construction of this stately coastal fortification, built using more than 25 million "Savannah Gray" and "Rose Red" bricks, was completed in 1847. This valuable defensive position, which looks like a truncated hexagon, consisted of a moat, parade ground and two powder magazines, would play a critical role in the Civil War.

Early in the war, the Union Navy blockaded the Confederate coastline in an attempt to cut all foreign trade and economic aid to the South. Fort Pulaski protected Savannah's prosperous seaport and the smugglers who dared to run the Union guns to bring weapons, medicine and even liquor to the beleaguered Southern army.

There have been many ghostly sightings at Fort Pulaski over the years. One particular encounter is relevant to our discussion because it appears to have involved a very "commanding" interactive ghost.

In 1861, Confederate militia under the command of Colonel Charles H. Olmstead occupied Fort Pulaski, located on Cockspur Island. In the spring of 1862, Federal troops under the command of General David Hunter, landed on nearby Tybee Island unopposed by the Confederates who watched from 8000 yards away. Over the next two months, Union troops positioned 36 pieces of heavy artillery on Tybee Island.

The resulting siege of Fort Pulaski would be the first real successful test of the Union Armies new rifled cannon and would lead to the eventual downfall of masonry fortifications in general. On April 10, 1862 General David Hunter began his bombardment of Ft. Pulaski. This artillery barrage would continue non-stop until the afternoon of April the 11th.

Even though there had been no Confederate casualties, Colonel Olmstead knew it would only be a matter of time before the Federal troops breached the walls of the fort. Seeing no other option, Colonel Olmstead surrendered Fort Pulaski to General Hunter later in the day. As the captured Confederate soldiers marched out of Fort Pulaski, they probably felt like they had let the citizens of Savannah down because they were supposed to have protected them from the Federal Troops.

In 1864, 550 Confederate prisoners were held at Fort Pulaski under the watchful eye of the Union troops garrisoned there. While incarcerated at the fort, these heroes of the Confederacy, would endure starvation, scurvy, and crippling dysentery. 537 prisoners would walk away from their prison alive when they were transferred to Fort Delaware a year later. The remaining 13 prisoners would die at Fort Pulaski, their bodies ravaged by emaciation and dehydration.

In the late 1980's, Savannah was again be occupied by both Federal and Confederate troops. These Civil War re-enactors were involved in the filming of the movie "Glory", which starred Morgan Freeman, Mathew Broderick and Denzel Washington, and was shot on location at various locations around Savannah. One group of re-enactors took advantage of some of their free time, and visited Fort Pulaski while en route to the movie set. While these modern day Civil War soldiers were exploring the fort, a young man wearing a Confederate lieutenant's uniform approached them. This young Confederate officer began to reprimand the re-enactors for not saluting him upon his approach. The lieutenant then ordered the re-enactors to fall into formation because a Yankee attack was imminent.

The re-enactors wanted to put on a show for any other visitors in the fort at the time, and decided to follow the lieutenant's commands. The lieutenant ordered the re-enactors to face about (turn away from him), which they did without question. This was the last time they would ever see the brash Confederate officer again. According to the re-enactors, the young man just disappeared and was never seen again.

FORT LEATON, TEXAS

In 1848, Ben Leaton, a reputed scalp hunter for the Mexican Government, built Fort Leaton on the abandoned site of a Spanish mission. El Apostol Sabriago, the first mission on the site, had been built in 1684. This adobe place of worship, later named El Fortin De San Jose was abandoned in 1810 and used as a private residence. When Leaton arrived in 1848, he purchased the old mission and began building his legacy of bloodshed and violence.

Ben Leaton, who had gained a reputation for his hospitality and his ability to get along with the local Indians, built an adobe homestead that encompassed a large courtyard and contained more than 100 Spanish style rooms. Though Fort Leaton had walls, a guardhouse, and lookout positions, it was always considered a private residence. Various military units would visit Leaton while exploring the frontier or chasing Indians, but it was never officially garrisoned by military troops.

There appears to be some debate about exactly how Ben Leaton got along so well with his Indian neighbors. It was often noted that the Indians living in the area never seemed to bother Leaton and that he seemed to have established a rapport with them. Later, this unwritten understanding between Leaton and the native population would be attributed to his sale of guns and ammunition to renegade Indians. But could Fort Leaton's fragile frontier tranquility be attributed more to "fear" rather than illegal commerce?

According to legend, when Leaton first arrived, he held a peace counsel at Fort Leaton with the local Indians. The next morning, following the peace talks, Leaton arose and found that Indians had stolen every horse and mule he owned during the night. Leaton knew that he could not let this encroachment go unpunished. He then set about a devious plan and later invited the Indians back for more talks. Once his Indian guests were seated for dinner, Leaton excused himself from the table and left the room. Unknown to all but Leaton, a cannon had been pointed into the room. It fired; spraying those assembled with canister shot. Armed men firing into the crowd from nearby rooftops killed any one who survived the initial blast. It is unclear if this story has any basis in fact, but it could explain why the Indians never bothered Fort Leaton.

In 1851, Leaton died of yellow fever. His wife later married Edward Hall. Apparently, Hall was not a financial wizard. Using the fort as collateral, Hall arranged two mortgages through John Burgess, an old friend of Leaton's. When Hall failed to make good on his debts; Burgess foreclosed demanding that Hall leave the fort immediately. Hall refused to leave the premises, and two assassins allegedly hired by Burgess, killed him in the fort. In 1877, Burgess himself, was gunned down by William Leaton in retaliation for his step-fathers death.

In 1926, The Burgess family abandoned the fort and homeless families later used it as shelter. In 1968, the Texas Parks and Wildlife Department acquired the property. Prior to the Texas Parks and Wildlife Department taking custody of the dilapidated mission, treasure hunters had scoured the ruins, and had dug a large pit looking for gold that Leaton allegedly buried in the fort before he died. Two park employees assigned to clean out this treasure pit reportedly fled the fort in terror after they claimed that they felt something invisible trying to pull them into the hole.

Other park employees have reportedly observed the transparent figure of Edward Hall in the same room where he was shot to death at the dinner table. An elderly woman, possibly the ghost of Mrs. Hall or Mrs. Burgess, has been observed several times by park employees sitting in a rocking chair in the fort's kitchen. And even today, it is rumored that during thunderstorms, a headless specter, a victim of a freak equestrian accident, rides around the fort's corral on a white horse. The moral of this little vignette is this... if you ever find yourself caught in a sudden thunderstorm near Fort Leaton, be afraid, be very afraid.

FORT WASHITA, OKLAHOMA

In 1841, the U.S. Army, under the command of General Zachary Taylor, constructed Fort Washita near modern day Madill Durant, Oklahoma.

Though considered isolated even by frontier standards, Fort Washita was constructed in order to establish law and order in the southeastern territories and to protect the Choctaw and Chickasaw Indian tribes from rival Indian tribes. The fort contained a large stable and corral to support the cavalry and dragoons, who frequently patrolled the plains to protect Indian and settler alike from raiding Comanches.

At the start of the Civil War, in 1861, Federal troops abandoned Fort Washita. Confederate soldiers operating in the area would later use the fort as a major supply depot and hospital facility during the war. When the Department of the Interior assumed control of Fort Washita in 1870, it was considered obsolete. Instead of reactivating the fort, the Department of the Interior deeded the property to a Chickasaw Indian named Abbie Davis Colbert and her son.

In 1962, the Oklahoma Historical Society purchased the buildings and grounds of Fort Washita. Extreme weather conditions and neglect left its mark on the post over the years. At the time the fort was purchased by the Oklahoma Historical Society, many of the buildings had collapsed or were in drastic need of repair.

In 1965, one of the graves in the post cemetery was exhumed. Imagine everyone's surprise when two bodies were found inside, one old, and one not so old. Forensic evidence revealed that the older (original) body belonged to a sixteen-year-old boy who had died of meningitis. More puzzling was the fact that the boy's skull had a deep gash near the temple. It was determined that newer body was that of an unidentified Hispanic male whose body had been hidden in the boys grave many years later.

The most unique spirit said to inhabit Fort Washita is that of "Aunt Jane". It is unclear exactly who Aunt Jane was, or how she died. Over the years, several stories about Aunt Jane's untimely demise have been handed down from generation to generation. Each time her story has been told, it is further embellished making it extremely hard to validate. However, it is possible that she was killed at the fort some time between 1842 and 1861.

One story suggests that Aunt Jane was a free Negro that had come to Fort Washita during the Civil War to spy on its Confederate occupants. It is said that when the Confederates uncovered Aunt Jane's true identity and mission, she was summarily executed by beheading, and her body and head were buried in separate graves.

The second story is a contradictory variation of the first. In this version, Aunt Jane, is actually a white woman. The influential wife of an officer stationed at the fort, Aunt Jane was rumored to have always carried $20 dollars in gold with her, no matter where she went. One day while returning from town, bandits who wanted her gold reportedly accosted her. In the ensuing struggle, the one of the bandits allegedly cut off Aunt Jane's head

The third account of Aunt Jane's murder involves a love triangle. As in the second account, Aunt Jane is the wife of an officer stationed at Fort Washita. One night, her husband returned home from a patrol and found his beloved in bed with another soldier who was also stationed at the fort. In a fit of rage, Aunt Jane's husband set upon the two lovers and beheaded them both on the spot. Later, the husband threw the heads of Aunt Jane and her lover in the Washita River.

Even though the possible causes of Aunt Jane's death are open to some debate, the nature and timing of her frequent appearances are not as suspect. The ghost of Aunt Jane is said to search for her head and or her hidden cache of gold only on the nights of the full moon in the months of March and October.

Today, visitors and historic re-enactors have reported strange encounters with the ghosts of Fort Washita. In one instance, two female members of a living history group were spending the night in the Bonahan cabin, west of the fort. On this particular evening, one of the women claimed that she was suddenly disturbed from her slumber by the sensation that she was being strangled.

A few hours later, the second woman awoke and reported that she could sense an invisible presence hovering over her. On the second night, a third woman joined the two re-enactors. The very next morning, each of the women reported that they had been plagued during the night by dreams involving suffocation.

FORT MONROE, VIRGINIA

The last military post we will visit is Fort Monroe. During the War of 1812, the United States learned that it was ill-prepared to defend its eastern coastline from the advancing British army. In 1814, the necessity for adequate coastal defenses was exemplified when Washington D.C. was captured and burned by the British. As a result of this embarrassing incident, a new coastal defense system was put in place. Fort Monroe would be the first of these new fortifications, its mission, to protect the entrance to Hampton Roads.

The construction of Fort Monroe was started in 1819. In 1609, the first English colonists built Fort Algernourne on the same site. As early as 1608, Captain John Smith realized that military defenses were needed to defend the approaches to the colony at Jamestown. The same site would be used as a defensive position throughout the colonial period. In 1834, Fort Monroe would be completed, and in 1824, it would become the Army's new Artillery School of Practice.

At the start of the Civil War, Fort Monroe's armaments and defenses were quickly improved to protect it from possible Confederate attack. The fort would serve as the starting point of several land operations against the Confederate army.

During World War II, Fort Monroe bristled with an impressive complement of coastal artillery guns, long range cannons and a series of rapid-fire weapons. Many of these advances in weapons technology were soon obsolete when the potential of the long-rang bomber and aircraft carrier was realized at the end of the war. Today, Fort Monroe serves as the headquarters for the U.S. Army Training and Doctrine Command.

Besides being an ultra modern military post, Fort Monroe is also the home of an alleged "Moat Monster" and is reputedly haunted by several famous people such as President Abraham Lincoln, President Ulysses S. Grant, Jefferson Davis, Chief Black Hawk and Edgar Allan Poe. Several other, lesser known, ghosts are also said to haunt the post as well.

It is hard to believe that one ghost can haunt so many different places, but apparently President Lincoln is the exception to the rule. His spirit is said to haunt a room in the fort's officers quarters. When observed, the visage of President Lincoln is seated at a desk, apparently deep in thought. When President Lincoln is off skulking around the White House or another famous location, his seat is kept warm by the phantom of President Ulysses S. Grant.

Jefferson Davis, the one time president of the Confederate States of America, is said to haunt the Fort Monroe prison. During his incarceration at the post prison, Jefferson Davis was forced to live like an animal in unbearable conditions. One day, he reportedly challenged one of his captors, and was beaten unmercifully. Later, Jefferson Davis would die as a result of his injuries. To this day, there have been several instances where the spirit of Jefferson Davis and the apparition of his dead wife, Varina Davis, have been observed in his cell.

A famous section of Fort Monroe, aptly titled “Ghost Alley”, is the home of the Woman in White and a spirit who can’t stand roses. We begin with the marriage of a beautiful young woman to an army officer nearly twice her age. The husband’s varied duties and assignments apparently kept him from his younger mate, and she found solace in the arms of another man. As in the previous story about “Aunt Jane”, the husband of this woman came home one night and found her in bed with the rival for his affections.

The husband quickly ran off the other man, but in a fit of jealous rage, murdered his wife. The Woman in White is said to haunt Ghost Alley, presumably in an attempt to be reunited with the spirit of her illicit lover.

At another residence located along “Ghost Alley”, the angry essence of an unknown entity is said to haunt the home of an army officer. This unseen presence apparently has a great disdain for roses. When past residents have left bouquets of roses anywhere in the home overnight, this malevolent energy scatters the petals all over the floor by the next morning.

But don’t think that officer’s quarters are the only places haunted at Fort Monroe. The ghost of a toddler is said to haunt basement of an enlisted soldier’s home. Occupants of the residence have heard phantom laughter in their basement and report that this mischievous spirit likes to hide their children’s toys. The identity of the child ghost and the cause of his or her death have never been determined.

CONCLUSION

As stated previously in this chapter, no one really knows what ghosts are. Many theories abound as to the origin of ghosts and spirits but it is an accepted belief that when several environmental and psychic factors are combined under the right circumstances, a location such as a military post or fort could become haunted.

The spirits that skulk around Fort Washita are typical of “Residual” manifestations that play themselves over and over again like a worn out video or audio tape. Ghostly phenomena such as the commanding lieutenant found at Fort Pulaski is "Interactive" in nature because the living people directly influence their actions.

Could all of the posts detailed in this chapter really be haunted? I do not know the answer to that question. However, based on a combination of theories presented in this chapter, there is a strong possibility that each of the military posts could be haunted. Each of these sites was constructed out of stone, adobe or brick. When you include the unbelievable number of personal trials and tribulations experienced by soldiers at each post over the years, it is easy to see how these factors, when combined, could serve as a valid reason why supernatural entities are encountered at each site.

And so, without further ado, let us begin our journey of discovery that will help us to truly understand the "Ghosts of Jefferson Barracks".

CHAPTER THREE

THE HISTORY OF JEFFERSON BARRACKS

Historic Jefferson Barracks, located on the high bluffs along the west bank of the Mississippi River, south of St. Louis, has served as a silent sentinel at the "Gateway to the West" for over one hundred and seventy five years. In that time, historical fact and legend have been woven into a colorful tapestry that makes this picturesque military post a true national treasure.

With the signing of the Louisiana Purchase, the vast untamed western frontier was opened for settlement. Jefferson Barracks, selected because of its strategic and geographical location, served as a way station and protector of explorers, traders, and pioneers seeking to establish a new life along the Santa Fe Trail.

Besides providing protection from marauding bands of hostile Indians, this prominent military reservation spanning over 1700 acres, served as a Army Infantry School, an influential Federal Hospital facility, a Engineer

Jefferson Barracks,
Aug. 1st. 1833

THOSE of the enterprising and able bodied citizens of Missouri and Illinois, who may be disposed to enrol themselves in *The New Regiment of U.S Dragoons*, now in organization, "for the more perfect defence of the Frontiers," can do so by applying to the undersigned, at Jefferson Barracks.

The term of service is fixed by law at three years, most of which will be consumed on, and beyond the frontiers, in the neighborhood of the Rocky Mountains. All necessary expenses, such as clothing, food, horses, forage and medical attendance, will be furnished by the Government; in addition to which the following rates of pay will be allowed to the Dragoons, viz.

	Pay per month.	Pay per annum.	Pay for 3 years.
	dols.	dols.	dols.
To the Sergeant Major, Quarter-master Sergeant, Chief Musician, and Chief Bugler—each,	16	192	576
To the First Sergeant of a Company,	15	180	540
All other Sergeants—each,	12	144	432
Corporals,	10	120	360
Buglers,	9	108	324
Farriers and Blacksmiths,	10	120	360
Privates,	8	96	288

R. HOLMES
Capt. U. S. Dragoons.

Example of the First Regiment Dragoons Newspaper Advertisement.
The First Dragoons were organized at Jefferson Barracks on March 4, 1833
(Courtesy of Tony Fusco)

Depot, a Calvary Training Depot, and one of the military's largest induction and demobilization centers in the United States. Over time, Jefferson Barracks was viewed as such a valuable resource in the training of soldiers and officers, that the military academy at West Point was almost moved there.

Prior to the 1900's, Jefferson Barracks was a key "stepping off point" for troops and supplies bound for distant conflicts such as; the Black Hawk Indian Wars, the Mexican War, the Civil War and the Spanish American War. Soldiers fighting in World War I and World War II were also trained at and deployed from Jefferson Barracks.

Considered to be the first permanent military installation west of the Mississippi River, Jefferson Barracks was a prison to Chief Black Hawk and several of his sub chiefs. Many years later, during World War II, Jefferson Barracks would again see itself become an internment camp for over four hundred German and Italian (Axis) prisoners of war.

During its heyday, Jefferson Barracks played host to a number of great leaders that would later influence American History. Three of these men, Dwight D. Eisenhower, Zachary Taylor, and Ulysses S. Grant rose through the military ranks and became future presidents of the United States. One young lieutenant, Jefferson Davis, even went on to become the president of the Confederate States of America. Several other young lieutenants and captains assigned to the post, such as Robert E. Lee, William T. Sherman, James Longstreet, and Winfield S. Hancock, saw their military careers culminate in generalship during the Civil War.

Jefferson Barracks would see itself flicker and fade into the history books one last time shortly after World War II. On June 30, 1946, this icon to the American ideal of "Manifest Destiny" was deactivated and declared military surplus. One hundred and thirty five acres of the main post was taken over by the Missouri Air National Guard and five hundred acres of the military reservation would be turned into an historic park by the St. Louis County Parks and Recreation Department.

Today, Jefferson Barracks is home to units from the Missouri Air National Guard, the Missouri Army National Guard, and the U.S. Army Reserve. The following highlighted segments of Jefferson Barracks's history will serve to give the reader a snapshot of the post; it's defining moments, and its eventual decline. For a more complete chronology of the history of Jefferson

Barracks please refer to the appendix at the end of this book.

FORT BELLEFOUNTAINE

Before Jefferson Barracks, there was Fort Bellefountaine. Established in 1805, shortly after the signing of the Louisiana Purchase, Fort Bellefountaine greeted the first pioneers and settlers heading west into the new frontier. Considered by the Army to be one of it most remote posts, Fort Bellefountaine was constructed north of St. Louis, near the confluence of the Mississippi and Missouri Rivers. This fort provided crucial military protection for St. Louis and its booming fur trade along the Mississippi Valley.

By 1826, Fort Bellefountaine had fallen into a state of disrepair and was considered unhealthy, due to the side effects of frequent flooding. When not fighting Indians or keeping the peace, soldiers fought with each other. On at least one occasion, a fellow officer killed a lieutenant during a duel and there was no indication that the situation would improve. It was eventually decided that Fort Bellefountaine was going to be abandoned. On March 4, 1826, Colonel Henry Atkinson was assigned to find a more suitable location for a new military base of operations in the West.

ESTABLISHMENT OF JEFFERSON BARRACKS

It did not take long for word to spread that the Army was looking for a new home. The villagers of Carondelet, saw the construction of a military reservation near their town as a golden economic opportunity for their small farming community. A short time later, a representative from Carondelet solicited Army officials in regards to the sale of 1702 acres of land south of the village for the new post.

On July 8, 1826 representatives from the U.S. Army and the Village of Carondelet met one last time to conclude the sale of the purposed property. After all parties signed a handwritten deed, a spokesman for the U.S. Army gave a single five dollar gold coin to a member of the delegation from Carondelet, sealing the deal.

On July 10, 1826, almost before the ink had dried on the contract, four companies of the 1st Infantry Regiment arrived at future site of Jefferson Barracks. These troops, under the command of Major Stephen Watts Kearny, immediately set about construction of temporary fortifications. This newly established military post was tentatively named Cantonment Adams, in honor of President John Quincy Adams. On October 23, 1826 the name of the post would be officially changed to Jefferson Barracks, in honor of President Thomas Jefferson who had died on July 4, 1826.

Initially, General Atkinson had been directed to construct the buildings at Jefferson Barracks out of bricks. Additionally, if there was insufficient materials or soldier labor present to complete the project, quarters were to be built of wood. Upon review, General Atkinson could not find enough qualified brick makers amongst his rank and file, but what he did find, was a lot of limestone deposits at the base of the near by cliffs. Under the direction of Colonel Henry Leavenworth, the construction of Jefferson Barracks officially began. Many of the stone buildings, arranged in a "U" with the opening facing the Mississippi River, were completed in 1834. At the time, it was estimated that this ambitious military building project cost the United States government approximately $70,000 dollars.

Almost as soon as the first building phase at Jefferson Barracks was completed in 1834, it was evident that many of the original buildings needed renovation or replacement. Soldiers living in cramped quarters were faced with leaking roofs and infestations of rats, roaches and bed bugs. In some instances, ground water seeped through masonry brick floors, air circulation was poor, and in the case of the post's first hospital, the foundation walls and pillars could not even support the building's weight. This deterioration of facilities continued until the early 1840's. In 1843, a formal Board of Survey issued a report, calling for sweeping improvements to many key buildings and auxiliary structures on post.

Of key concern was the condition of the post's water supply. By 1839, water from nearby springs and wells was deemed unfit for drinking and cooking, by the post's surgeon. The surgeon suggested that river water should be used instead. This presented a problem in the summer when the river water was too warm. Taking this into consideration the post surgeon recommended that ice be issued to all troops. These observations by the post surgeon lead to the construction of the post's first "ice house" soon there after.

Jefferson Barracks saw its next major building phase during the Civil War. Three large, temporary, hospital complexes were established northwest of the parade ground. Following the Civil war, many of these hospital buildings were no longer needed and were torn down.

Work was started on the present-day Headquarters Building in 1900. This photograph shows a view of the building as it looked around 1909.

In 1892, the original limestone buildings would be demolished, and new brick buildings constructed in their place. These new quarters belonging to officers, non-commissioned officers (NCO's) and enlisted alike, were testaments to a new lifestyle brought about by the "Golden Age of St. Louis". These new facilities were equipped with every modern convenience available at the time. By 1900, most of this modernization was completed and work was started on Building 1, the present day post Headquarters. Many of these impressive red brick buildings are still in existence today, and are being used by guard units stationed at Jefferson Barracks.

THE INDIAN WARS

Almost from the first time the white man set foot upon the New World, their ideals and the ways of the Native Americans already living here, came into conflict. As a result, once proud Indian tribes were forced from their land by white settlers and were required to move farther and farther away from their homelands. The Louisiana Purchase may have been a windfall for the fledgling United States but it spelled disaster for the Native

Americans.

The Indian now saw the settler as an invader and the frequency of Indian attacks increased throughout the Mississippi Valley. In 1832, Chief Black Hawk, Chief of the Saukie Indian Tribe refused to relocate his people to new lands west of the Mississippi River. Troops from Jefferson Barracks were ordered to restore peace and move against Chief Black Hawk and his rebellious tribe.

The resulting Black Hawk Indian War ended in 1832 when Chief Black Hawk and several of his sub-chiefs were captured after the Battle of Bad Ax River. A young Lt. Jefferson Davis was assigned to escort Chief Black Hawk and his sub-chiefs back to Jefferson Barracks, where they were incarcerated for a short time. Chief Black Hawk would later be jailed at Fort Monroe and on a Indian reservation in Iowa.

Chief Black Hawk would live to be 71 years old. During his imprisonment, he wrote his autobiography, toured the eastern seaboard and even had an opportunity to meet President Andrew Jackson. On October 13, 1883, Chief Black Hawk died while he was still being incarcerated for his pivotal role in the Black Hawk Indian War.

In 1836, troops from Jefferson Barracks marched against the Seminole Indians in Florida during the Seminole Indian War. The state of war which existed between the Seminole Indian's and the United States government would not be officially settled until 1925 when both parties signed a formal treaty of peace.

Even after the Civil War, infantry and cavalry units from Jefferson Barracks were constantly vigilant in their efforts to protect travelers and settlers from Indian raids. The true measure of service these frontier soldiers provided to the early citizens of the West can be summed up with one statistic. Between 1850 and 1890, soldiers from Jefferson Barracks participated in over 13,000 separate campaigns against the Indian tribes in the western territories.

A SOLDIERS LIFE AT JEFFERSON BARRACKS

"No Sergeants, Corporals, drummers, fifers, or private soldiers, are to appear in the barrack-yard, or street, without their hair being well plaited and tucked under their hats: their shoes well blacked, stockings clean, black garter, black stocks, buckles bright, and cloathes in thorough repair."

THE MILITARY GUIDE FOR YOUNG OFFICERS, 1776, P.234

A member of the U.S. military assigned to Jefferson Barracks today enjoys a vastly different lifestyle than his or her predecessors did. During the 21st century, the modern soldier on post would consider power outages, plumbing and air conditioning woes and computer network "crashes" as wholly unacceptable working conditions. To the first soldiers stationed at Jefferson Barracks, these would be considered child's play.

Life on the early frontier was fraught with both manmade and natural dangers. Summer time brought excessive heat and humidity that when combined pushed temperatures near the 100 degree mark on almost a daily basis. This extreme heat and vast array of flooded marshes along the Mississippi Valley brought another problem, in the never-ending waves of mosquitoes and other germ-carrying flies. These pesky little bloodsucking insects were especially veracious in the areas along the riverways where the larva hatched. At the other end of the weather spectrum was winter. The blustery cold season may have brought soldiers relief from the heat and mosquitoes, but with it came wind chills and freezing temperatures. Soldiers who were billeted in unhealthy quarters and exposed to these varied conditions were always more susceptible to a host of epidemic diseases such as cholera, yellow fever and small pox.

Wild game, deer, bear, buffalo and other smaller edible animals, were in great abundance in and around Jefferson Barracks in the early days. So much so, that it is said that an early post commander had to issue an order forbidding enlisted soldiers to shoot at buffalo on the parade ground because the bullets that missed their targets were hitting the officer's quarters. The number of times soldiers intentionally missed their mark is debatable but nevertheless, I am glad that I was not a company commander back then.

The early soldier's formal military training at Jefferson Barracks consisted primarily of practice in the manual of arms on the parade field. Some time was spent on weapons familiarization, bayonet drill and target practice, but there were scarcely enough supplies of powder or shot to supplement this rudimentary training with any real tactical experience.

A typical day for a cavalry soldier included weapons drill in the morning and mounted or dismounted drill on a circular track called the "Bull Ring" in the afternoon. The real veterans in camp were born out of encounters with hostile Indians on the frontier, not from a drill book.

For the most part, garrison duty was dreary and monotonous. When not performing drill and ceremonies, soldiers at Jefferson Barracks were assigned to guard mount, fatigue duty, and provided for the general maintenance of the cantonment's buildings and grounds. When not assigned to extra duties, most soldiers of this time period were left to their own devices. This included fighting, drinking, liaisons with prostitutes and of course dueling.

DUELING

Though not officially sanctioned by the U.S. Army, dueling was commonplace at Jefferson Barracks in the 1830's. On January 19th 1830, 2nd Lt. Charles O. May, a member of the 6th Infantry, lost his life in a duel with a fellow officer near the north gate of Jefferson Barracks. Also in that same year, Major Thomas Biddle, post paymaster and Pettis Spencer, a congressional candidate, killed each other with pistols in a duel at the post.

These tests of honor frequently occurred on post, but they also took place on Bloody Island. Aptly named, Bloody Island, located in the center of the Mississippi River, opposite St. Louis, had been the site of many famous duels. One notable duel that is known to have occurred on Bloody Island even involved a future president of the United States, Abe Lincoln. By 1838, Bloody Island became land locked to the Illinois shore as a result of the successful efforts of Captain Robert E. Lee to channel the Mississippi River. However, this marvelous feat of engineering did little to curb incidents of dueling between the officers stationed at Jefferson Barracks.

Time and time again, it became obvious that dueling was draining the officer corps at Jefferson Barracks of promising young leaders. This needless loss of life prompted military commanders to issue proclamations that stated that the continued practice of dueling would bring harsh reprimands and punishment for all persons found to be involved in this kind of activity.

DISCIPLINE

The early U.S. colonial Army was heavily influenced by many of the foreign officers that saw it through the Revolutionary War. With these British, French and Prussian officers came the misguided idea that "Discipline" would be the foundation of the new military order in the United States. These same ideals would become the mainstay of garrison life at many military posts along the western frontier.

Incidents of drunkenness and desertion were the most common offense perpetrated by enlisted men at Jefferson Barracks. On average, 50 to 60 soldiers each year were court-martialed at the post for these kinds of violations. In most cases, soldiers who were found guilty were reduced in rank and required to pay some fine. Continued violations on the part of the soldier would see them lose their whiskey ration for twenty to thirty days at a time.

By the late 1880's extreme measures of discipline and outlandish levels of punishment for petty infractions were a fact of life for soldiers stationed at Jefferson Barracks. Soldiers were abused, cursed at, threatened, and bullied by strong-arm tactics that put the fear of god into the common enlisted man. Medical services provided on post were virtually non-existent and in many instances, food and meat were put out on the mess tables the night before, making it inedible for the soldiers the next day. This not so glamorous aspect of camp life lead to over 300 desertions from Jefferson Barracks alone, between July 1, 1888 and June 30, 1889. This equaled to about one disgruntled soldier leaving Jefferson Barracks almost every day that fiscal year.

Men who could not adjust to military life at Jefferson Barracks deserted the army by several different means. Some hid on trains that had stopped at the Jefferson Barracks train depot, some escaped by swimming the Mississippi River, and some even fled in boats. One particular soldier devised a foolproof plan to get out of the army. He dressed himself as a civilian and walked nonchalantly out the front gate. The army paid $30 dollars for each deserter captured and returned to Jefferson Barracks.

It is said that one early oppressive commander at Jefferson Barracks had the ears cut off two soldiers who had deserted the army. For this unnecessary inhuman act, the officer was later fined one months pay, but in most cases, it was the soldier who suffered.

Deserters who had been recaptured were thrown into the post stockade or military jail. Once in the stockade, soldiers experienced truly harsh and sadistic punishment. Prisoners in confinement were exposed to cramped, foul and filthy living conditions that were infested with swarms of bed bugs. To add insult to injury, prisoners were also subjected to physical torture by being hanged by their thumbs and from being shackled in leg irons for little or no reason.

In June 1889, Frank R. E. Woodward enlisted in the United States Army. Private Woodward was assigned to Jefferson Barracks, Company B, Calvary Depot, for training. Normally a private enlisting in the military would not cause much of a fuss, but in this instance it created one of the most interesting episodes in the history of the post.

Private Woodward was an undercover reporter for the *St. Louis Post Dispatch* newspaper, who had enlisted into the army to learn the reason why so many soldiers from Jefferson Barracks were deserting from the post. Private Woodward would experience camp life first-hand. He found the soldier's living quarters infested with bedbugs and learned that mess sergeants were stealing the soldier's food and transporting it off post. This criminal activity Private Woodward learned, was causing frequent food shortages on post.

In one report, Private Woodward told the story of a Black soldier who was beaten to death by a NCO who found him sitting in an area that was considered off-limits to Black soldiers. Private Woodward did not personally witness the assault, but he had witnessed NCO's and officers beat recruits during training so it was easy to understand why he would feel that a second-hand story of this nature had merit.

Private Woodward reported his observations directly to the newspaper, and his graphic exposé's became front-page news in St. Louis. These news articles would also become an embarrassment to many high-ranking officers at Jefferson Barracks. Due largely to Private Woodward's investigative reporting and the public outcry, the Army launched an investigation into the disciplinary practices and physical conditions at the post. The findings of the Army inquiry called for the physical reorganization of the post. Additionally, many of the officers involved were reassigned to other military installations and several NCO's found themselves demoted. Never underestimate the power of a lowly private.

The Post Hospital was constructed at Jefferson Barrack's around 1905.

ILLNESS AND EPIDEMIC

During its history, three great cholera epidemics descended upon Jefferson Barracks and the surrounding Mississippi Valley. With each passing plague, the post was clouded in sadness and death. Hundreds of soldiers died as a result of these cholera epidemics.

During one such cholera epidemic, there were so many deaths attributed to the disease, that a "Dead House" or morgue, was constructed at the northeastern corner of the present day parade ground, to house all of the remains. In 1834, twenty soldiers at Jefferson Barracks died of cholera. As a result of the outbreak of this dreaded intestinal tract disease, medical officers ordered the post and surrounding properties disinfected with chloride of lime.

In most cases, the cures the doctors provided to stave off these deadly diseases were almost as bad as the illnesses themselves. Soldiers experiencing a bout with cholera were given a chalky mercury compound called Calomel and large doses of Laudanum. As if these "wonder cures" were not dangerous enough, post surgeons also employed blood letting, a common medical treatment of the time, to combat cholera and other frontier diseases.

With the dawn of the early part of the 20th century, the Mississippi Valley would see the last major outbreak of smallpox and in the 1940's the post experienced an almost epidemic attack of spinal meningitis. This ravaging disease would take a grim toll on trainees and inductees assigned to the overflowing base.

DR. WILLIAM BEAUMONT

In 1835, Dr. William Beaumont became the post surgeon at Jefferson Barracks and served in that capacity until 1840. Dr. Beaumont had established himself as a prominent medical surgeon and scientist with the publication of his book, "Experiments and Observations on the Gastric Juice and the Physiology of Digestion."

Even though he was sometimes considered controversial, Dr. Beaumont was actively involved in the creation of the Medical Society of Missouri. However, in 1844, Dr. Beaumont's fame and glory would be tarnished by a scandalous malpractice lawsuit involving an indigent patient named Mary Dugan. Originally, Dugan was a patient of Dr. Stephen Adreon. Dr. Beaumont came into the picture when he was consulted in regards to a tumor on the right side of Dugan's groin. It was alleged that Dr. Stephen and Dr. Beaumont had misdiagnosed Dugan's affliction and that she had been disabled as a result of these two doctor's negligent surgery skills. Almost overnight, the case became a media spectacle in St. Louis. The case went to trial in 1846, but in the end, a jury cleared both Dr. Adreon and Dr. Beaumont of any wrong doing in the matter.

THE MEXICAN WAR

Before the U.S. Congress officially declared war with Mexico on May 13, 1846, U.S. and Mexican troops had clashed on at least four occasions. Much of the hostility between the U.S. and Mexico had been precipitated much in part by the massacre of Texans at the Alamo, by Mexican troops under the command of General Santa Anna.

The first real confrontation between Mexico and the United States occurred on April 25 1846, when Mexican troops crossed the Rio Grande and attacked a unit of U.S. Dragoons. This fray, though relatively minor by today's standards, was eighteen days before any formal declaration of war had been announced. Between May 3rd and May 9th 1846, U.S. troops and Mexican regulars faced each other again during the Siege of Fort Texas, also known as Fort Brown. This engagement only served to fuel the flames of war. The subsequent Battles of Palo Alto on May 8 1846, and Resaca De La Palma on May 9 1846, brought tensions to a head, causing congress to formally declare war against Mexico on May 13, 1846.

During the Mexican War, Jefferson Barracks served as a staging area for troops and equipment headed to the war. After adequate preparations had been made, infantry, militia and mounted units were transported to the war zone by steamboat while other would travel overland to Santa Fe, New Mexico.

The young men who enlisted in these various military units did so more out of a desire to seek glory and adventure rather than out of a sense of patriotism. Money certainly was not a big factor in attracting these recruits. If he survived unsanitary camp conditions, disease and the primitive battlefield medical techniques practiced at the time, a private in the Army could expect to be paid $8.00 dollars a month for services rendered to his country. In one case, a group of Missouri volunteers under the command of Colonel Alexander Doniphan had to wait over twelve months before they would see any money at all.

The Mexican War tested many soldiers and their leaders. Many of these young, brash lieutenants, such as Braxton Bragg, Sterling Price and James Longstreet cut their teeth in various battles during this conflict. Some of these officers would live obscure lives while others rose through the ranks, to see service again, as future generals during the Civil War.

By the time the war was brought to a close by the signing of the Treaty of Guadalupe Hidalgo, on February 2, 1848, almost 30 million square miles of land were added to the United States. Soldiers returning to Jefferson Barracks following the war were "mustered" out of the service and back into the civilian world.

THE DRED SCOTT CASE

In 1834, Dr. John Emerson, an Army surgeon stationed at Jefferson Barracks, purchased a slave named Dred Scott from the Blow family of St.

Louis. At the time of the transaction, slavery was an accepted aspect of life in Missouri.

Shortly after purchasing Scott, Dr. Emerson took him on various military assignments to Illinois and the Wisconsin Territories. Even though these areas prohibited slavery, many military officers felt that these laws did not pertain to them. These Army officers considered slaves to be their property and transported them freely through territories that prohibited this kind of barbaric activity.

While abroad with Dr. Emerson, Scott met Harriet Robinson, another slave, and took her as his wife. In 1842, Dr. Emerson would return to St. Louis with the Scott's, but not before Mrs. Scott had given birth to a baby girl on free soil. Shortly after returning to St. Louis, Dr. Emerson died. Scott sued for his freedom from Dr. Emerson's widow in 1846, by entering a petition in the circuit court of St. Louis.

The Old St. Louis City Courthouse, standing at the corner of Chestnut and Market Streets would become the stage for this most unusual lawsuit. Scott and his lawyer, Francis Murdoch argued that since Dr. Emerson had taken Scott to live on "Free Soil", he should be granted his freedom. The court did not see the situation in the same manner and Scott lost his initial lawsuit.

In 1850, a determined Scott took his case to court again. This time Scott was successful but the victory was short-lived. In 1852, the Missouri Supreme Court reversed the lower court's ruling based on an appeal by Mrs. Emerson. On November 2, 1853, Scott and his lawyer Roswell Field, were in court again. Only this time, Scott and Field brought their case to the United States Circuit Court in St. Louis. Scott failed to win his case and the Federal court upheld the previous lower court's ruling against him. Scott and his lawyer appealed the Federal court's ruling to the United States Supreme Court. At stake, the constitutionality of the Missouri Compromise.

The United States Supreme Court, dominated by staunch southern supporters, heard arguments on Scott's case in 1857. As with the previous court battles, Scott was denied his freedom, but in doing so, the Supreme Court ruled that the Missouri Compromise was unconstitutional. This paved the way for slavery in all of the remaining territories.

On May 26 1857, Scott's new owner, Taylor Blow, set Scott and his family free. Dred Scott died a free man on September 17, 1858, and was buried in Calvary Cemetery in St. Louis.

This case was monumental in the fact that it fractured public and political opinion in regards to the divisive issue of slavery, eventually leading to the Civil War and the signing of the Emancipation Proclamation.

THE CIVIL WAR

At the start of the Civil War, the total strength of the U.S. Army was less than 17,000 soldiers. Since most of these "regular" soldiers were stationed as various locations around the United States and the Indian Territories, the core of America's fighting force was heaped upon individual state militias. Prior to 1861, Jefferson Barracks was the Headquarters for the Department of the West, and up until the opening shots of the war, there were not many military units that had not been assigned to Jefferson Barracks at one time or another.

As the early battle lines of the Civil War were being drawn in 1860, sympathies between the North and South were very closely divided in Missouri. These political and military divisions worked to tear Missouri apart at a critical time in the state's history. Through all of this unrest, Jefferson Barracks and the Federal Arsenal in St. Louis remained stalwart bastions of the "Republic", firmly supportive of the Union Army, and of the ideals of President Abraham Lincoln. As the threat of war loomed on the horizon, military operations at Jefferson Barracks kicked into overdrive.

When Confederate forces bombarded Fort Sumter in Charleston Harbor on April 12, 1861, Jefferson Barracks was thrust into the war as an important training base for Missouri's Union volunteers. Men and equipment began to pour into Jefferson Barracks from a variety of sources. Troops and supplies arrived and departed the post by steamboat, train, and by other various over land routes.

Early Federal preparations for war in the St. Louis region were so feverish that the roads to Jefferson Barracks became inundated with militia, Cavalry, artillery, and Regular Army unit's on the march to assemble at the post. To compound the confusion, thousands of volunteers desiring to join the army of the "Republic" flocked to the post.

By May 1861, Captain Nathaniel Lyon and William T. Sherman had learned that militia troops sympathetic to the Southern cause, camped at Camp Jackson, were intending to attack the Federal Arsenal at St. Louis.

Without formal orders, Captain Lyon took the initiative.

"The Burial of a Comrade"... A number of funerals took place on the post during the Civil War era, as seen in this 1909 postcard.

On the morning of May 10 1862, Federal troops, including units from Jefferson Barracks, the Federal Arsenal, and a St. Louis militia organization, encircled the pro-southern militia quartered at Camp Jackson, in St. Louis. This show of Federal might, convinced D.M. Frost, the Camp Jackson garrison commander, to surrender without a fight. Captain Lyon's quick action, magnified by the support of the men and material from Jefferson Barracks, undoubtedly ensured that Missouri remained a part of the Union, but the day would not end without blood being spilled on the streets of St. Louis.

While en route back to the Federal Arsenal, Federal troops escorting the Pro-Southern prisoners from Camp Jackson along Olive Street, was encircled by an angry crowd. The volatile situation spun out of control, and shots were fired. Who actually fired the first shot is still a mystery. What is known, is that after the first shots rang-out, nervous Federal troops reacted as if in combat, and fired into the assembled crowd. When the smoke had cleared, scattered amongst the moaning wounded in the street, were almost three dozen dead. Sadly, most of these casualties were civilians. Due to the civil unrest and riots in St. Louis, General John C. Fremont, Commanding

General of the Department of the West, declared Martial Law in the city on August 8, 1861

A more humorous incident occurred in 1862, when a steamboat bearing of all people, Samuel Clemens (Mark Twain) was fired upon by Union soldiers as it passed Jefferson Barracks. A gun emplacement that had been set up on the bluff behind the post headquarters fired upon the steamboat, which was attempting to run the blockade at Jefferson Barracks. The steamboat, its passengers, and crew, survived the ordeal but the vessel's smokestacks had two holes blown through them as a result of its encounter with the Federal battery.

JEFFERSON BARRACKS CIVIL WAR HOSPITAL

As the Civil War entered its second year, Jefferson Barracks would see its role in the war change from that of an armed camp, to that of an influential Federal medical facility.

By March 1862, it was clear that the Civil War was consuming more and more resources of men and materials. This created a need for more hospitals to treat the sick and wounded. By the fall of 1862, the Army Medical Department had built nine temporary, one-story medical buildings at Jefferson Barracks. Combined, these new medical facilities had the capacity to house 3000 patients. Also during this time, the Western Sanitary Commission built a large hospital also capable of housing up to 3000 injured soldiers, at the post.

Injured troops from Carthage, Boonville, and Springfield, Missouri were transported to the barracks as were wounded from distant battlefields around the United States. These patients were transported by hospital railway car and by the hospital ship fleet of the U.S. Navy, which used the docks at Jefferson Barracks as a base of operations.

Most military and field hospitals during the Civil War were grotesque places. Many times these primitive medical facilities were grossly overcrowded, and they were places where ignorance and disease were the real killers. Here, soldiers faced a daily battle with germs, rudimentary childhood diseases such as chicken pox, and worst of all, gangrene.

After the Civil War, medical procedures improved nationwide. Facilities at Jefferson Barracks were considered better than most, but in some instances, it was reported that several men were permanently crippled or disfigured due to the total disregard of their well being by the post surgeons. In Private Woodward's newspaper articles (1889), he reported that the post hospital was in good condition and that the food served to patients was also of good quality. However, Private Woodward noted that the physicians at sick call displayed a "callous attitude" towards their patients.

Those soldiers who did not survive their convalescent stay at Jefferson Barracks, were buried in the National Cemetery, established south of the post in 1863. A separate chapter in this book further describes the history of the Jefferson Barracks National Cemetery in more detail.

THE SPANISH-AMERICAN WAR

As the massacre of Texans at the Alamo by troops under General Santa Anna pulled America into the Mexican War in 1846, the sinking of the Battleship *USS Maine* by an underwater mine in the Havana Harbor propelled the United States into the Spanish-American War on April 25,1898. As in the Mexican War, and the Civil War, Jefferson Barracks served as an induction point and training area the Missouri National Guard and militia units from several different states. In their fervor to join the army, soldiers from many volunteer militia and National Guard units arrived in their civilian clothes because they could not afford military uniforms or equipment. Military records for that time period indicate that the average soldier was 27.6 years old at the time of enlistment.

Men from all walks of life heeded President McKinley's call to arms. This spirit of patriotism even included men of color. Four units made up almost entirely of Black soldiers were formed at Jefferson Barracks to fight in the jungles of Cuba.

These special units were formed because it was thought at the time that the Black soldiers were immune from the yellow fever and typhoid that was taking its toll on their white counterparts who were also being deployed to the war zone. Following the Civil War, Black units were traditionally led by white officers. During the Spanish American War, Black soldiers were allowed to obtain the rank of lieutenant but segregation of military units would exist until after the Second World War.

On August 12 1898, the war with Spain came to an end. Of the 3549 United States casualties during the war, including the service men killed on the *USS Maine*, 2957 deaths were attributed to disease.

Victorious troops returning from Cuba, Puerto Rico and Manila, arrived at Jefferson Barracks, where they were mustered out of Federal service. In 1899, Jefferson Barracks was presented with a cannon recovered from the Spanish battleship *Oquenda* which was sunk on July 3, 1898, in Santiago Bay. Today, visitors to Jefferson Barracks can still see this prized trophy which is located on the bluff, directly behind the post headquarters.

The gun from the Spanish battleship Oquenda can still be seen overlooking the river behind the post Headquarters Building.

WORLD WAR I

In 1915, prior to the "War to end all Wars", troops from Jefferson Barracks took part in the Mexican Punitive Expedition. This military operation under the command of General John J. "Black Jack" Pershing, was organized to capture "Poncho Villa" who had been conducting bandit raids into American territory.

As the tide of war raged across Europe in 1914, the United States sat on the sidelines watching. American's would watch in awe as the Germans to bombed Paris and towns in England using Zeppelin air ships and as German submarine "Wolf Packs" continued to send tons of men and machines to the bottom of the ocean. Increased attacks by German submarines on merchant vessels sailing to and from the United States, would eventually draw the country into the fray.

On April 6, 1817, the United States formally declared war on Germany. With this proclamation, Jefferson Barracks was pressed into service as the country's largest induction site. Soldiers deploying from Jefferson Barracks arrived in Europe and were suddenly thrust into the landscape of modern warfare. These "Dough Boys" would cross the Atlantic Ocean, patrolled by aggressive German submarines, and find themselves in mud soaked trenches, face to face with ominous tanks, devastating machine guns and the large-scale employment of chemical munitions.

During the World War I era, a street car station was located near the Post Office and the Post Exchange

In July 1918, the German's made a last ditch effort to mount an offensive against the Allies. This attack commenced near Mezy, France, along the Marne River. Facing the German onslaught, were soldiers from the 30th and 38th U.S. Infantry Regiments. Most of these brave young men would see combat for the first time at the Battle of the Marne. For many, it would be their first and last time. In the end, the U.S. troops repelled the German attack and made a counter attack possible.

Following the signing of the Treaty of Versailles on June 28 1919, Jefferson Barracks would again become the countries preeminent demobilization site for troops returning from overseas.

WORLD WAR II

The unprovoked Japanese attack of Pearl Harbor on December 7, 1941 launched the United States into World War II. On December 8, 1941, Jefferson Barracks saw some military action as well. At the start of hostilities, all furloughs were cancelled and sentries were posted at key locations on the base. Soldiers were ordered to fire at any person who failed to stop upon command. This lead to the indiscriminant attack upon a milk truck, in the opening days of the war. This incident occurred when nervous sentries opened fire on the truck and its driver when the vehicle would not stop at the front gate.

During the Second World War, Jefferson Barracks served primarily as an induction and separation center, and later become the largest technical training school for the Army Air Corps. Many of the soldiers who were sworn into military service at Jefferson Barracks later completed basic training at the same location. It is estimated that more than 400,000 soldiers from the U.S. Army and other military branches were processed and trained at Jefferson Barracks between 1941 and 1944.

The North Gate of the Post as it looked in the 1940's

The outbreak of the Second World War caused the population of Jefferson Barracks to increase ten-fold. With this steady increase of raw fighting testosterone in the St. Louis metropolitan area, post medical personnel started to see a corresponding increase in the number of cases of venereal disease.

A crack down on vice and prostitution by the St. Louis City Police Department brought about a drastic, but welcome, drop in the number of venereal disease cases treated by doctors on post.

Of the thousands of soldiers who inundated Jefferson Barracks during the Second World War, not all of them were there on their own accord. Over 400 of these new occupants were German and Italian (Axis) prisoners of war.

During the flood of 1943, Axis prisoners helped to fill sand bags, standing side by side with their captors from Jefferson Barracks. These same prisoners later participated in a work strike in 1945, laying down their tools in protest over the way a fellow prisoner was disciplined. The rebellious strikers were given bread and water for several days. Hunger encouraged the prisoners to go back to work peacefully. By the end of the war, seven of these prisoners would die at Jefferson Barracks. Their bodies were laid to rest in the National Cemetery.

One of the Tent Camps at Jefferson Barracks during World War II

THE CLOSING OF AN ICON

On June 30, 1946 the United States flag was lowered one last time at Jefferson Barracks, during final retreat. Of the original 1700 acres, the Missouri Air National Guard acquired one hundred and thirty five acres for use as a training site. The War Department declared the remaining acreage as "surplus".

In the years that followed, The remaining property comprising the old military reservation fell into a shameful state of decay. Vandals and souvenir hunters scouring the site only served to speed up the deterioration of the boarded up, unattended buildings. A sigh of relief was heard in 1950, when the St. Louis County Parks and Recreation Department acquired 500 acres of this "surplus" land to establish the Jefferson Barracks Historic Park. Today, the Jefferson Barracks Historic Park boasts quite an array of modern athletic fields, picnic shelters, an amphitheater, and several museums dedicated to this historic location.

For over one hundred and seventy five years, Jefferson Barracks has directly and indirectly influenced the military history of our nation. Its very construction at the "Gateway to the West" ensured that the early American dream of "Manifest Destiny" would become a reality. Through the years, great men such as Ulysses .S. Grant, Robert E. Lee, William T. Sherman, Zachary Taylor, and Dwight D. Eisenhower served at Jefferson Barracks. These prominent men and many more like them in the fields of politics and medicine have given a part of themselves to the history of Jefferson Barracks through their individual deeds and accomplishments.

Last but not least, the history and grandeur of Jefferson Barracks is a testament to the literally hundreds of thousands of soldiers who have passed through its gates over time the post has been in existence. The sacrifices and personal experiences of these men and women will not go unheard. Could this be the reason why so many ghosts seem to haunt this historic location? Unfortunately, we may never know the answers to that question until we have passed on to the other side ourselves.

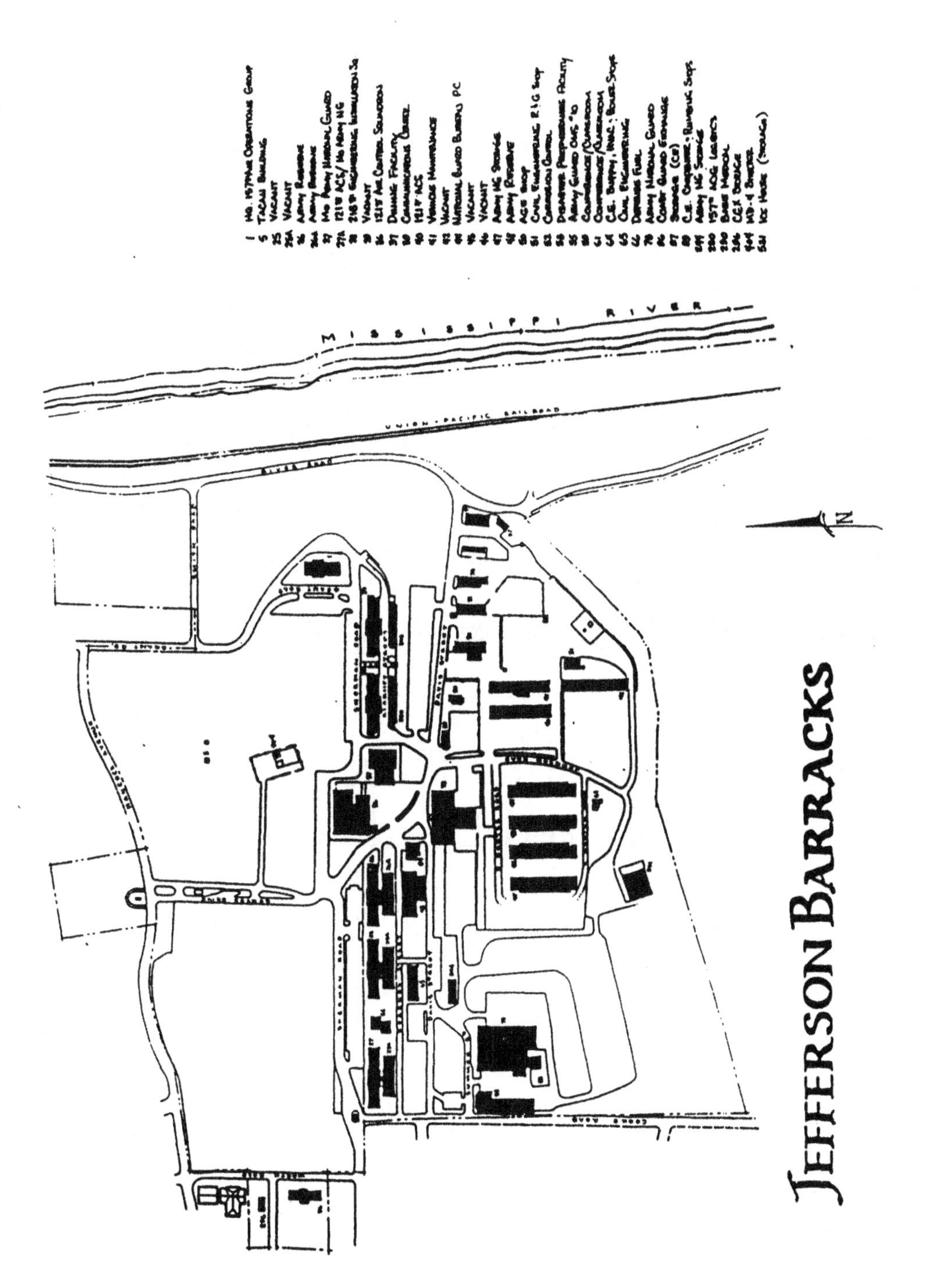

Map of Jefferson Barracks (courtesy of John Sonntag)

CHAPTER FOUR

JEFFERSON BARRACKS NATIONAL CEMETERY

Missouri's Resting Place for Its Honored Dead

The muffled drum's sad roll has beat
The soldier's last tattoo:
No more on life's parade shall meet
That brave and fallen few.
On Fames's eternal camping-ground
Their silent tens are spread,
And Glory guards, with solemn round,
The bivouac of the Dead
THEODORE O.'HARA (1820-1867)

One cannot visit The Jefferson Barracks National Cemetery and not be moved both physically and emotionally. As you walk between the seemingly never-ending rows of marble headstones, bleached by the relentless Missouri sun, you can literally sense that the spirits of those enshrined there, are watching you. The feeling is sobering yet unreal because you come across so many graves that are marked 'Unknown'. It is particularly haunting because if you suspend your disbelief for just moment, it seems like you can almost hear the voices of the dead on the wind. Are the multitudes of the "Unknown's" crying out to be recognized even after death?

HUMBLE BEGINNINGS

When Colonel Henry Atkinson established Jefferson Barracks, in October 1826, a section of land was set aside along the southern edge of the post for a small burial ground. Here, soldiers and their family members who had the misfortune to pass away while stationed at Jefferson Barracks were laid to rest overlooking the meandering Mississippi River. A wooden fence was erected around this hallowed place in a vain attempt to keep out wild animals. Soldiers assigned to Jefferson Barracks were detailed to perform basic upkeep and maintenance of the cemetery. The existing post commander usually determined how the cemetery was maintained, in the absence of any standards dictated by higher headquarters. In the end, it would remain the responsibility of the dearly departed's friends and family to provide care for a specific gravesite.

With the reassignment of soldiers and their families, the unattended graves of loved ones were left behind and over time, the graveyard degraded into a state of unrecognizable disrepair. As the cemetery expanded years later, these old forgotten memorials were relocated but by that time, the identity of the entombed were in most cases forgotten and unidentifiable.

The remains of those found under these circumstances would be reinterred in the cemetery with only a number or the word "unknown" carved on the head stone. What a way to be remembered.....

If you visit the Old Post Section of the Jefferson Barracks National Cemetery, you will notice that this section stands out from the whole. Here, large, elaborate memorials can be seen intermingled with formalized headstones added later. As there were no set standards for the cemetery in the beginning, family and friends were allowed to construct whatever sized monument they could afford. When this small necropolis's status was upgraded to that of National Cemetery, a strict set of standards was put in place. The days of the large, ornamental headstones in the cemetery had come to an end.

Today, the Jefferson Barracks National Cemetery encompasses over 300 acres of property that was at one time part of the original military reservation. In the next few pages, you will learn how this relatively insignificant cemetery, known as the Old Post Cemetery, was later tapped and expanded over the years to become the fourth largest National Cemetery in the country.

THE FIRST BURIALS

On August 5, 1827, Elizabeth Ann Lash, the eighteen month-old daughter of an army officer stationed at Jefferson Barracks, had the notable distinction of being the first person buried at the Old Post Cemetery. Very little is known about the Lash family or the cause of young Elizabeth's death. It is plausible to think that this poor child, brought into this world at a military citadel on the edge of civilization, could have fallen ill and died as a result of any of a number of mysterious epidemic diseases that were ravaging the Mississippi Valley at the time.

The second person buried at the Old Post Cemetery was 2nd Lieutenant Charles Copeick. A member of the 6th Infantry Regiment, 2nd Lieutenant Copeick was laid to rest next to the grave on Elizabeth Lash on January 9, 1828.

On January 19, 1830, 2nd Lt. Charles O. May, a member of the 6th Infantry, was also laid to rest in the Old Post Cemetery. 2nd Lt. May's death is notable because he was the ultimate loser in a duel with a fellow officer that had taken place near the north gate of Jefferson Barracks. Little is known about the other principal, his name, his health after the confrontation, or why these two gallant officers decided to solve their grievance in this manner. At the time, dueling was not an official army institution but it occurred with frightening regularity when men of honor perceived another had wronged them. In the end, strict orders were issued implying that harsh reprisals would be meted out to all parties involved if this preposterous practice continued.

THE CIVIL WAR

By 1862, it was clear that more burial sites would be needed to inter the remains of those soldiers who died fighting in battle during the Civil War. To add to the increased demand, even more plots were needed for those Civil War soldiers who passed away in hospitals or who died while incarcerated as prisoners of war. Major General Henry W. Halleck, commander of the Department of the Missouri, recognized that Jefferson Barracks was an excellent choice for a national cemetery because of its strategic location, and the availability of port facilities for paddlewheel steam vessels.

In 1863, based on Major General Halleck's initial observations, President Abraham Lincoln, by power of Executive Order, expanded the "Old Post Cemetery" and created a National Cemetery. In 1866, The United Stated Congress formally recognized and designated the "Old Post Cemetery" as the Jefferson Barracks National Cemetery.

From its very inception, the hastily laid out burial plots at the newly established Jefferson Barracks National Cemetery started to fill up at a mind-boggling rate. The remains of soldiers, from both the North and South, started to arrive at Jefferson barracks for burial. U.S. dead from Civil War battlefields around the country were transported by all means imaginable to Jefferson Barracks where they were staged pending burial in the cemetery.

As previously noted, Jefferson Barracks played a key role during the Civil War, serving as a military hospital for the sick and injured soldiers of the Northern Army. Considering that these medical facilities and the training of the medical personnel, who manned them, would be considered crude by today's standards, many of the soldiers, who were sent to the hospital at Jefferson Barracks to recuperate, later succumbed to their injuries or from complicating infections. These soldiers too, were buried at the National Cemetery.

A CIVIL WAR INJUSTICE

To add to the list of the fallen buried at the National Cemetery, six Confederate soldiers, selected at random from the prisoner population at the Gratiot Street Prison in St. Louis, were executed on October 29, 1864. The execution, ordered by General William Rosencrans, St. Louis Provost Marshal General by Special Order No. 279, took place at Fort #4, south of Lafayette Park in St. Louis. General Rosencrans ordered the execution of Private Asa V. Ladd, George T. Bunch, James W. Gates, Charles W. Minnekin, Private John A. Nichols, and Private Harvey H Blackburn, in retaliation for the massacre of Major James Wilson and six union prisoners on October 3,1864, following the Battle of Pilot Knob. Of the six marked men, only Private Blackburn had taken part in the Battle of Pilot Knob.

When the six Confederate prisoners arrived at Fort #4, they were greeted by a 36~ man firing squad, comprised of soldiers from the 41st Missouri and 10th Kansas Infantry. It was evident that some of the soldiers assigned to the grim detail were reluctant to perpetrate this outrageous act. The commander of troops told the assembled soldiers that it was their duty to carry out their orders. The execution detail swallowed their apprehension, and the rest is history. As a result of this unjust act, six motionless bodies hung incredulously on poles at the center of the execution ground.

The dead Confederate prisoners were transported to the Jefferson Barracks National Cemetery where they were buried in adjacent graves, section 20, graves 4605 to 4610. In the end, the bodies of more that 1,140 Confederate soldiers were interred at the National Cemetery in Sections 19, 20, 21, 22, 66 and 67. To make matters worse, these sons of the Confederacy are joined at the National Cemetery by over 12,000 of their Union brethren.

(Left) "A Civil War Injustice" The Graves of the men executed at Lafayette Park

THE YEARS FOLLOWING THE CIVIL WAR

On November 25, 1867, Mr. Sylvanus A. Beeman, formerly a Sergeant in the Union Army, was appointed as the first Superintendent of the cemetery.

In 1868, Mr. Martin Burke was installed as the second Superintendent of the cemetery. Under Mr. Burke's watchful eye, the grounds were improved, and the cemetery was divided into sections for ease of identification.

In April 1876, 470 graves were moved from Arsenal Island also known as Quarantine Island, and reburied at the Jefferson Barracks National Cemetery. The age-old powerful currents of the Mississippi River had formed Arsenal (Quarantine) Island. Located just north of Arsenal Street in St. Louis, the island was a half a mile wide and three quarters of a mile long. Arsenal Island served as a sort of "mini Ellis Island", where soldiers suspected of being infected with contagious diseases, such as small pox, cholera, and yellow fever were held in quarantine. Steamboats bearing various military units and civilian passengers were directed to Arsenal Island when they arrived in St. Louis. When they reached the island, medical surgeons inspected the passengers to insure that no one was infected with a contagious disease that could spell disaster for the St. Louis region if it were allowed to spread to the civilian population.

Those passenger's who were believed to be infected with cholera, small pox, or yellow fever, were forced to live on the island until they were deemed healthy, recovered from their illness or died. Those who died were buried at the north end of the island. In 1866, the city of St. Louis purchased Arsenal Island and continued to use it as quarantine.

Over time however, Mother Nature was Quarantine Island's worst enemy. By 1880, surveyors in St. Louis had recorded that the island had slowly shifted approximately 4, 800 feet down river. This was nearly a mile from the island's position in the channel when it was surveyed in 1862. Frequent spring flooding washed away many of the graves and markers of the deceased. As a result, human remains were routinely scattered in the Mississippi River between St. Louis and New Orleans. In 1876, the remaining graves on the Quarantine Island were finally moved to the Jefferson Barracks National Cemetery. As the names and identities of those people buried on Quarantine Island were also washed away in the spring floods, those remains reinterred at the National Cemetery, were identified with new tombstones that were marked 'Unknown'.

In August 1866, 175 noncommissioned officers and men of the United States Colored Infantry died due to complications from cholera. An obelisk, erected in Section 57, 15009 of the cemetery, commemorates their service to the United States.

On April 12, 1900, Superintendent Burke died. His successor, Mr. Edward Past, became the third Superintendent of the cemetery. Originally, grave markers in the cemetery were made of wood. Over time, the wooden markers became weathered and unreadable.

In 1873, marble headstones replaced the old wooden markers. The gravestones of Union soldiers had rounded tops and were embossed with an inlayed shield. The stone markers of the Confederate dead had distinctively pointed tops and the sunken shield was omitted. While serving as Superintendent, Mr. Burke was responsible for swapping out the unreadable wooden headboards for the new marble ones.

A monument to the remains that were moved from old Fort Bellefountaine to the Jefferson Barracks National Cemetery in 1904.

On April 5, 1904, the remains of those (33) officers, soldiers and family members who had been buried at Fort Bellefountaine between1806 and 1826, were moved to the National Cemetery. These “Unknown’s” including the two year-old daughter of Lt. Zebulon Pike were reburied on the same bluff, near the grave of Elizabeth Lash. The St. Louis Chapter of the Daughters of the American Revolution erected a large memorial, consisting of a granite boulder and commemorative plaque, at the site.

OTHER GREAT CONFLICTS BIG AND SMALL

Following the Spanish American War, approximately 200 unknown remains were reinterred in Sections 233, 34, and 45 of the National Cemetery. The graves of the courageous "Dough Boy" who died fighting in World War I, are located in Sections 41,46, 47, 50, and 51. Buried with these fallen heroes of Battles such as the Argone, and the Belleau Woods, lay approximately 250 "Unknown" soldiers.

During another 'Great War', World War II, Jefferson Barracks served as a Detention Camp for over 400 German prisoners of war. Two German prisoners and five Italian prisoners died while they were incarcerated at Jefferson Barracks. Their bodies were buried at the National Cemetery in Section 57 ½, alongside Congressional Medal of Honor recipients and countless soldiers from around the globe.

On December 14, 1944, 123 American Army and Navy personnel who were prisoners of the Imperial Japanese Army, on Palawan Island in the Philippines, were crowded into an air raid shelter. Once there, their captors poured gasoline on them and put them to the torch. A formal investigation into this matter after the fact, revealed that the unfortunate prisoners who were able to escape, were massacred by Japanese soldiers waiting outside of the shelter.

On February 14, 1952, the remains of these servicemen were disinterred from their original graves on Palawan Island and reburied at the Jefferson Barracks National Cemetery. This gravesite, located in Section 85, is the largest single mass grave at the cemetery.

MASS GRAVES

Many group burials at the National Cemetery consist of the remains of one or two soldiers who were buried in the same location. These relatively minor groupings of remains that were interred in a common gravesite were considered a group burial. These group burials and a larger number of war dead and "Unknowns" are buried at the cemetery, in more that 557 mass burial sites. There are more mass burials at the Jefferson Barracks National Cemetery than at any other cemetery in the country.

In addition to these mass graves, there are 46 memorials located in

Section 83, commemorating those soldiers who were buried at sea, cremated, or who's bodies were donated to science. 3,255 "Unknown" soldiers buried at various different locations in the National Cemetery join these dead but not forgotten warriors in their eternal rest.

MEDAL OF HONOR RECIPIENTS

I would be remiss in my duties as chronicler of historical fact and ghostly lore if I did not identify the Medal of Honor Recipients buried at the Jefferson Barracks National Cemetery and the locations where their remains are interred.

Major Ralph Cheli: Section 78, World War II Group Burial, Graves 30-934.

Lieutenant Commander Bruce VanVoorhis: Section 79, World War II Group Burial, Graves 270-272.

1st Lieutenant Donald Pucket: Section 79, World War II Group Burial, Graves 279-281

1st Lieutenant Lorenzo D. Immell: Section 4, Grave 11450.

1st Sergeant Alonzo Stokes: Section 63, Grave 11450.

Sergeant Henry M. Day: Section 65, Grave 11798.

Today, it is estimated that over 103,000 service men and women have been buried at the Jefferson Barracks National Cemetery. The cemetery is ranked fourth out of over 114 National Cemeteries in the United States based on an average of over 3,500 interments annually. It is estimated that over 13,000 veterans in Missouri alone, die each year and that on any given day, 10 or more soldiers are laid to rest in the National Cemetery.

On July 1, 1999, the Missouri National Guard created the Funeral Honor Program. I have personally worked with many of the men and women who provide this selfless service and I salute them for honoring the veterans and their sacrifices to this nation. It is estimated that once filled to capacity, the Jefferson Barracks National Cemetery will contain beneath its hallowed ground, approximately 500,000 of America's martyrs for freedom. These men and women have made the ultimate sacrifice for their country. I would say that in total, this is a final mark of distinction for an Old Post Cemetery which in 1826, was considered to be at the far edge of the Western frontier.

For more information regarding this historic location, you can contact:

Jefferson Barracks National Cemetery
2900 Sheridan Road
St. Louis, MO 63125
(314) 260-8720

The Gates to the National Cemetery as they look today

CHAPTER FIVE

THE GHOSTS OF JEFFERSON BARRACKS

One could reasonably argue that, per square acre, Jefferson Barracks is the most haunted location in the St. Louis metropolitan area. The post is comprised of one hundred and thirty five acres containing forty-one buildings of various shapes and sizes. Of those forty-one buildings, military and civilian employees occupy thirty-five of these, at any given time. Most of the occupied historic buildings serve as administrative offices, classrooms and maintenance facilities for the varied national guard and reserve units stationed at the barracks, while some of the structures are used primarily for storage. The six remaining buildings stand vacant awaiting asbestos abatement.

Of those thirty-five "occupied" buildings, thirteen or more have stories of paranormal activity associated with them that I am aware of. I am sure that if truth were told, there are more personal ghost stories out there that are waiting to be unearthed.

Over the years, soldiers and civilian staff working at Jefferson Barracks have reported a wide array of ghostly phenomena. Even Private Woodward, during his undercover time of service, reported that ghost stories seemed to abound at Jefferson Barracks. These brushes with the supernatural range from the phantom footsteps associated with residual hauntings to incidents involving interactive phantoms.

The stories you are about to read come from various locations inside the current military reservation. A separate chapter has been devoted to "Off Post Haunts". Each tale has been grouped under the building or location where it allegedly occurred. I think that you will find, as I did when compiling this information, that no one story or encounter you read about in the following pages is really like the next. But in the same respect, each account has one thing in common, they will leave you feeling unnerved.

I believe that a Lieutenant Colonel who currently works at Jefferson Barracks said it the best, " If you have ever worked late in one of these old buildings, you would be convinced that ghosts exist".

EARLY GHOST STORIES

Over the last 175 years, countless ghost stories have been told and retold about Jefferson Barracks. As the years passed, each new generation of storytellers embellished these simple campfire stories until they rose to the level of local folklore and legend, such as is the case with the spirit of a Civil War soldier who is said to appear during times of national crisis.

Due to the verbal heritage of many of these ghostly legends most cannot be bolstered by any supporting factual information. Sadly, in some instances, many of these early stories were never written down and have been forgotten forever.

One of the few people, who have made it their life's work to preserve the history and legends of Jefferson Barracks, is Technical Sergeant Tony Fusco (Retired). In August 2001, I had the distinct pleasure to interview Mr. Fusco. Without a doubt, he was one of the most interesting people I had the pleasure to meet with.

Mr. Fusco has written several books on the history of Jefferson Barracks and the National Cemetery. He has been actively involved in the Jefferson Barracks Historical Society and played a pivotal role in seeing that the barracks is preserved as a historic treasure.

When I was doing research for this book, I actively sought out and read *The Story of the Jefferson Barracks National Cemetery, the Pictorial History of Jefferson Barracks*, and *Historic Jefferson Barracks*, written by Mr. Fusco. Almost from the start, I was intrigued by two ghost stories he mentioned in his compilation of articles found in *Historic Jefferson Barracks.*

When I ask Mr. Fusco about these stories, he smiled and admitted that they were interesting little stories that he had collected through the years, and they were aptly used in his article titled "Facts and Legends of Jefferson Barracks". Mr. Fusco could not say where the stories originated from or if they had any basis in fact. You will get an opportunity to learn more about these ghostly tales in the following pages.

BUILDING 1

Standing proudly at the eastern end of the parade field, high on a grassy hill overlooking the Mississippi River, is Building 1. Constructed in 1900, this three-story brick building serves as the post's headquarters. The large room on the south end of the second floor was used as a ballroom. Many of the ornamental wood fixtures still exist there today. On the north wall of the old ballroom hangs a large, wooden, hand painted map of Jefferson Barracks, which was painted by an army private in 1938.

Recently refurbished to its former glory by the Missouri Air National Guard, Building 1 plays host to a multitude of ghostly encounters that have taken place both inside and outside of the building. One such entity frequently seen at Building 1, is that of an elderly Confederate Civil War general who has been observed in the post commander's office.

Sergeant William McWilliams, currently assigned to the Funeral Honors Program as a Team Leader, has probably had the most hair-raising encounter with this ghost to date. When Sergeant McWilliams first started as an employee of the Funeral Honors Program in 1998, he was living in Building 78 (one of the haunted buildings we will discuss later in this chapter) One night, Sergeant McWilliams was bored and decided to jog around the post to get some exercise.

Sergeant McWilliams admitted that he was somewhat out of shape and that he stopped near the display cannon from the Spanish battle ship *Oquenda* located behind Building 1, to catch his breath. While recuperating from his physical exertion Sergeant McWilliams observed what he believed to be candlelight coming from an office on the first floor, near the north end of the building. This odd light piqued Sergeant McWilliams's curiosity because there were no other lights on in the building, so he approached hoping to determine its source.

What he found to be the source of the light, was not what he expected in the least. As he got closer to the window, Sergeant McWilliams caught a glimpse of an older man, wearing what he believed to be a Confederate general's uniform and slouch hat, seated at a desk inside the post commander's office. The "old general" appeared to be writing dispatches with a feather quill pen. As Sergeant McWilliams watched in stunned silence, the solitary figure sat quietly working. The immediate area around the "old general" was illuminated by a single candle sitting on the desk. Sergeant McWilliams watched the Civil War-era officer in awe for three or four minutes before the figure finally rose and walked toward the door of the office with his feather quill in one hand and the candle in the other. As the old officer neared the doorway, he simply faded away into nothingness, right in front of Sergeant McWilliams startled eyes. Needless to say, out of breath or not, Sgt. McWilliams did not stick around to see if the "general" reappeared.

Several other employees working in Building 1 have observed a shadowy ghost of a man who sits at desk near a window on the second floor of the building, dispatching written orders by candle light. It is possible that this is also the ghost of the "old general" but we may never know. When the employees attempted to investigate the second floor while the phantom was present, all they would hear or see upon their approach, were the sounds of footsteps walking away.

According to Sergeant McWilliams, restless spirits are also active in the basement of Building 1 as well. When the Funeral Honors Program was first established at Jefferson Barracks their office and training area were located in the basement of Building 1. As part of funeral honors training, soldiers were required to practice with a full-sized casket, which was stored in the basement. Sergeant McWilliams said that every morning, he would walk into the funeral honors training area, and he would find the casket lid open and that it looked like someone, or something, had "rummaged" through the training items kept inside.

Another person who has had first hand experience with the spirits inhabiting Building 1 is Security Officer Richard Dickson. Working for the Missouri Department of Public Safety, Officer Dickson has been assigned to Jefferson Barracks for the last ten years of his law enforcement career.

Officer Dickson recounted an unusual experience he had in Building 1 one evening. On this particular night, he was working by himself and he had entered Building 1 to get a soda from the vending machine in the basement. After getting the his soda, Officer Dickson walked back up to the first floor and noticed that when he reached the open landing, he could hear a typewriter randomly typing somewhere on the second floor.

This concerned Officer Dickson because he knew no one was working in the building and all of the lights in the building had been turned off earlier in the evening when the last employees had gone home for the night. When Officer Dickson started to walk up the landing towards the second floor to investigate the situation further, he noticed immediately that the typing abruptly stopped for no reason. Officer Dickson thought this was unusual but when he did not hear more typing he thought that maybe there was a natural explanation for the sound he had heard.

What happened next though, proved to Officer Dickson that the sound was caused by anything but something "natural". When Officer Dickson started to walk back down to the first floor, the typing mysteriously started again. According to Officer Dickson, this unexplained encounter with the unknown "freaked him out" and he immediately left the building, returning to the lighted safety of the "guard shack".

Several other Air National Guard employees working after hours in Building 1 have experienced some unusual paranormal events there as well. Employees report hearing ghostly footsteps when no one else is in the building, the sounds of chairs and furniture moving around by itself, and lights turning on and off by themselves. In one case, these noisy spirits caused such a racket, that the employee who heard the unnatural noises, turned up his radio just so he would not hear what was going on around him.

On one occasion in 1974, Master Sergeant Jerry Faust, Training Manager for the Missouri Air National Guard, had his own "spooky" experience while he was working in the basement of Building 1. Master Sergeant Faust will always remember this particular evening because that was the night that he started to hear heavy objects, thought to be boxes of paper, falling on the floor above. During normal business hours this was a common occurrence because a friend working in the copier room above would jokingly drop boxes of paper on the floor and then Master Sergeant. Faust would respond in kind by pounding on the ceiling. On this particular night, after hearing the noises from above, Master Sergeant. Faust went upstairs to see who was working in the copier room. When Faust dashed up the stairs to ascertain the source of the commotion, he found nobody working in the room, and everything appeared to be in its place. This series of events occurred several times in a row that same night and each time when Master Sergeant Faust investigated the causes of the noise, he found the area above his office undisturbed. After the fourth time Master Sergeant Faust heard "something" fall on the floor above his office, he thought it best to continue his work at home.

Prior to this experience, Master Sergeant Faust was never really bothered by the atmosphere of the building. Following his experience, he kept the incident to himself and decided not to tell anyone about it. "People just don't talk about these things, they try to brush it off," he explained. It was not until he was having a discussion with another officer who worked in the building, and the topic of hearing footsteps and other strange noises came up, that Master Sergeant Faust would finally tell his strange tale.

Master Sergeant Judy Jarvis, an Information Manager for the Missouri Air National Guard also encountered several unexplained situations in Building 1 after hours.

In the Fall of 1992, Master Sergeant Jarvis was working in her office, which was located on the first floor of the building near the main foyer, when all of a sudden, she started hearing several desks being moved around on the second floor of the building.

She described the second floor of the building as having tiles on the floor, which magnified the sound of the moving furniture. Initially, it was just the noise that was annoying to Master Sergeant Jarvis because other employees had talked about moving furniture around upstairs, and Jarvis just thought that night was the night they decided to move stuff around. As the noises continued, Master Sergeant Jarvis decided to investigate the situation further.

After yelling, "I'm leaving now", several times up the stairs, Master Sergeant Jarvis turned out all of the lights and locked the exterior doors of the building. When she got to the parking lot, she immediately observed that there were no other cars parked in the lot but hers. Master Sergeant Jarvis decided to re-enter the building to see if anyone was in fact inside moving furniture. When she unlocked the door and went back inside, she found the hallway light turned on, this was one of the lights she was sure was turned off when she left the building the first time. Jarvis said that she checked the entire building but never found anyone else inside and never found what was making the loud noises she heard earlier in the evening.

"I always have my doubts about the noises I hear because they can be explained as the normal noises of a shifting building." Master Sergeant Jarvis said, explaining that she has spent the night in Building 1 several different times. Of those times, she said that she had to leave only twice because of "an overwhelming need to get out of the building." This was apparently the case on this particular night, and Master Sergeant Jarvis decided it was in her best interest to collect the rest of her things and leave the building in all due haste.

Another time, Master Sergeant Jarvis was working in the building in the early afternoon when she heard the distinctive sound of a can of soda dropping out of a vending machine in the basement. Master Sergeant Jarvis went to the basement and checked to see if anyone was there. She found all the doors near the vending machines locked. At the time, only two other people were working in the building, and Master Sergeant Jarvis later learned that they had not purchased any soda that day.

Interestingly enough, even the large flagpole in front of Building 1 has a ghost associated with it. This grand flagpole with its ornamental cannon display, located just east of the parade field, is the focal point of many of the post's special events and activities. One night, an unnamed security officer was patrolling the grounds and conducting building checks. As the officer neared the east-end of the parade field, he observed a person sitting near the flagpole. As the officer drove by in the safety of his security vehicle, he continued to observe the mysterious person and noted that as he got closer, the person "seemed to disappear" right before his eyes. When the officer completed his rounds, he drove by the flagpole a second time, and observed the same mysterious stranger seated near the flagpole. According to an anonymous source, this ghostly encounter scared the officer so much that he would not come out of the security shack for the rest of the evening.

The ghost at the flagpole could be related to another transparent figure observed on the grounds behind Building 1 by soldiers during the Civil War.

Mr. Tony Fusco told me that during the Civil War. and the wars that followed, soldiers guarded the train depot and tracks located along the Mississippi River, below Building 1 and that armed guards also actively patrolled the grounds around the building.

In this instance, a Civil War sentry was walking his post around Building 1. When he walked behind the building, he observed a lone figure walking up the large grassy hill towards the building, from the train yard. As the soldier stood watching, he realized that the person was not a man at all, it was a transparent wispy "spook".

BUILDING 29

This large double barracks, was built in 1897. Limestone from the barracks that stood in its stead previously, was used as the foundation for the new troop quarters, which could hold up to four companies of soldiers. As was typical of the day, each unit's NCO's were housed separately from the enlisted soldiers, in a center section of the building that had three floors. Today, used as storage by the Air Guard, this building has its own story to tell

One guardsman has reported hearing ghostly footsteps walking down the hallway or running up the stairs of the Building 29 when no one else was present. The same soldier also heard toilets flushing when there are no toilets in the building, and that he even heard a mysterious voice say "dismissed".

BUILDING 290

Built directly behind Building 29, is Building 290. This two-story building, originally used as a mess hall, was completed in 1942. Currently, the building is used as an Air Guard base medical facility, but for several weeks in October 1985, this would be the same building where Gloria Barnes, a civilian working for the Base Civil Engineering unit, would have an encounter with something paranormal.

Ms. Barnes' daughter, who was two years-old at the time, had been enrolled in dancing lessons at a location near the post. For several weeks during that fateful October, Ms. Barnes would bring her daughter to her upstairs office after work, prior to dance class. While Ms. Barnes caught up on back-logged paperwork, her daughter would eat dinner or play quietly in the office. It was during this "quiet" time, when no one else was in the building, that Ms. Barnes started to hear things that could not be explained.

At first, she thought she heard someone moving around at the other end of the building. Upon closer inspection, Ms. Barnes found that all of the entrances and exits to the building were locked and that her car was the only one parked on the parking lot. A short time after returning to her office, Ms. Barnes started to hear foot steps at the other end of the building, where she had heard the other unexplained noises not moments before. Again, Ms. Barnes attempted to determine the source of the footsteps, but again she found that she was the only one in the building. Now more than a bit apprehensive, Ms. Barnes returned to her office, but almost immediately after she had started working on her paperwork again, she started to hear doors opening and closing down the hall.

This same series of events continued during the weeks that followed. Each time, Ms. Barnes found that she and her daughter were locked securely in the building, after every one else had gone home for the evening. She described this experience as definitely being "very creepy". At the conclusion of her daughter's dancing lessons, Ms. Barnes quit staying in the building after hours. Ms. Barnes summed up her interview by saying, " If you tell anyone from off-post these stories, they will look at you like you are crazy, but if you have ever spent any time at Jefferson Barracks at all, you know that there is some truth to the ghost stories you hear."

BUILDING 28

Situated right next to Building 29 is Building 28. Built in 1897, this double barracks, having a three-story center section, also held up to four companies of cavalry or infantry and each unit's NCO's. Today, this building is home to the 218th Engineer Squadron. Besides being of the same design and construction, Building 28 mirrors Building 29 in the fact that it too appears to have a residual ghost.

This vintage photo shows the Enlisted Men's Quarters (Building 28) as it looked in the early 1900's

One evening in the Fall of 1980, Chief Master Sergeant Eugene Anacker, and several other Air Guard NCO's, were working late in the building. After concluding their business for the night, the group turned out the lights, locked the doors, and met briefly in the parking lot across the street from the building. While talking on the parking lot, Chief Anacker noticed that a light on the third floor was on, and dispatched the lowest ranking NCO in the group to go back in the building to turn the light off. The young NCO unlocked the main doors, climbed the stairs to the third floor, and turned the light off. After the NCO locked the building and walked back to the parking lot, Chief Anacker looked back up at the building, and observed that the third floor light was on again. Thinking that faulty wiring in the old building could have caused the malfunctioning light, Chief Anacker again sent the young NCO back into the building to turn off the light.

When the NCO returned to the parking lot, Chief Anacker was shocked to see that the light on the third floor was shining brightly as if it had not already been turned off twice. So, again, the intrepid NCO was dispatched back into the building to turn out the light. When the NCO's returned to the parking lot the next time, no one looked back to see if the lights were on, instead, they just left as soon as possible.

Even prior to the mysterious turning on and off of lights in Building 28, Chief Anacker had heard ghostly footsteps in the building on several different occasions. In 1978, Chief Anacker had been staying late in the evening working on training records for an upcoming inspection, when he heard someone walking around on the second floor above his office. As Chief Anacker listened, he noticed that after awhile, it sounded like more than one person was walking around upstairs. Chief Anacker investigated the second floor to see who or what was making the noises but when he got to the location where he felt the noises were originating from, the "footsteps" had stopped. When the chief arrived back at his desk, the muffled footsteps started again. Chief Anacker knew for a fact that he was the only person in the building during each of the these encounters, but he was hesitant to tell anyone because, "people give you a funny look when you tell stories like this. I know what happened, I was there."

BUILDING 280

Built directly behind Building 28, much in the same manner as Building 290 was constructed behind Building 29, Building 280 was completed in 1942. Originally designed and used as a mess hall, today members of the 157th AOG Logistics unit use the building for office space.

In September 1995, Master Sergeant John Sonntag, Engineering Technician observed a reflection on the screen of his computer monitor that would defy explanation. Working late to complete a year-end funding projects, Master Sergeant Sonntag was working at his computer terminal in a desperate attempt to process as many projects as possible before the midnight deadline arrived. Master Sergeant Sonntag remarked that it was a quiet evening, and that if he looked out the south windows, he could see row upon row of headstones standing silently in the National Cemetery, just south of post.

As Master Sergeant Sonntag continued to complete project after project, he started to notice an eerie whistling noise coming from the area of the south wall, facing the cemetery. Thinking that it was just the wind, Sonntag continued to work at his computer, oblivious to the fact that the whistling was getting louder. So loud in fact that it again got Master Sergeant Sonntag's attention. Rising from his chair, Master Sergeant Sonntag walked to the window, but as he approached, the whistling noise suddenly stopped.

"I just could not get over how the whistling had just stopped when I moved to the window", commented Master Sergeant Sonntag. A short time later, Master Sergeant Sonntag went outside behind the building to smoke a cigarette and check the wind, "there was absolutely no wind at all and it gave me the Willie's because I couldn't figure out what was causing the whistling sound."

After finishing his cigarette, Master Sergeant Sonntag returned to his office and dived headlong into his last remaining project on his computer. By this time of the evening, Sonntag felt that he and the security officer at the front gate were the only people on post. Knowing that security officers will sometimes check buildings that have lights left on, he even expected that the gate guard would stop by and see him before he left for the evening.

The prior suspicious whistling noise all but forgotten, Master Sergeant Sonntag hunkered down at his keyboard, trying to make his deadline. Admittedly, not an accomplished typist, Master Sergeant Sonntag, frequently looked up at his computer monitor to check his work. It was during one of these quality control checks that Master Sergeant Sonntag saw the figure of a person standing behind him.

"As I looked up to the screen to check my work, I saw a shadow first block the light behind me on the left and then proceed past the shadow of my head and through the right side. I turned and looked over my right shoulder thinking that the gate guard would be standing there but he wasn't." Master Sergeant Sonntag started to dismiss the flickering image behind him on his computer monitor, but then he remembered the unexplained whistling sound that he had heard earlier in the night, and looked back at his computer screen again.

"When I looked back at the screen, the right side of the screen was shadowed and then it moved in behind my head. I sat perfectly still and the feeling of a light breath of air or a gentle touch started at the nape of my neck and brushed up the tips of my hair to the top of my head." Startled, Master Sergeant Sonntag jumped from his chair, spun around, but found nothing. Deciding that he could wait until the next day to finish his remaining project, Master Sergeant Sonntag collected his belongings and ran from the building. "I stopped at the gate house and asked the gate guard if he was messing with me and he just crinkled up his nose and looked at me like I was nuts." Needless to say, it was a night that Master Sergeant

Sonntag would never forget.

BUILDING 37

Just west of Building 28, situated across Johnson Road, sits Building 37. This building has an interesting history, which could lend some credence to why it is allegedly haunted today.

The first building constructed on this site was a “Reservoir Building”. Built around 1860, this large brick, two-story building served as the post’s “water works”. Water from the Mississippi River was pumped by steam engine to four large 1000-gallon water tanks, located on the second floor of the building. Water from these tanks was then dispersed to the other buildings on post through an intricate pipe system.

In 1883, the “Reservoir Building” was refurbished and it became the post’s guardhouse and jail. The rooms on the second floor were used to house the guard contingent and the duty officer. The first floor served as the jail.

According to several of Private Woodward’s undercover articles, this floor was separated into two rooms. One room, termed the “Garrison side” housed recruits who had committed general offenses. The second room, called the “General side”, contained an iron 20’ by 40’ cage, which was used to hold soldiers who had committed more dire acts on post.

At any given time, there were approximately 40 soldiers imprisoned in each room. Soldiers who were incarcerated on the “General side” either slept on the floor, or on bed slats without mattresses. Prisoners who were housed on the “Garrison side” slept in bunks or hammocks if the space was available. Both rooms were prone to flooding when the water tanks located above the guardhouse overflowed and were infested with swarms of bedbugs.

Building 37, as we know it today was built in 1897. Like the building that stood in its place before it, this building served as the post's new guardhouse and jail. During the early 1990's, the building was refurbished yet again. Today, the first floor of the building serves as the post's dining facility and the ground level is used by the Air National Guard as a Battle Management Training Center. Because of the building's history, it is not hard to believe that this former jail continues to house at least one ghost within its stone walls.

One morning, in 1992, a female Air Guard soldier had a frightening encounter with a smoky human form that seemed to float several feet off the floor. The soldier observed the transparent figure as it floated in front of her while she walked down one of the building's hallways. Based on her observations, the soldier guessed that what she had saw that morning was the ghost of a woman, because its clothes were flowing behind it. This chance encounter with the paranormal had an emotional affect on the soldier, who was moved to tears.

BUILDING 531

Built in 1941, this cement block building served as the icehouse for Jefferson Barracks. During World War II, this building, part of a group of warehouses at the southern edge of post, was used for cold storage. Two railroad spurs serviced building 531 and the other warehouses in that area. The building was later used for storage and as a maintenance site for civilians who were re-building historic military vehicles. Today, the building stands vacant.

Flanked by the rows of tombstones from the National Cemetery in the background, the building seems shrouded in an uneasy calm. It is said that on quite summer evenings, one can still hear the sound of men and equipment working in the vacant building, moving invisible blocks of ice.

BUILDING 78

Erected in 1912, Building 78, also known as Atkinson Hall, served as the post's main dining facility. Atkinson Hall, with its distinctive white-washed exterior, replaced the post's old dining facility, Building 36, which was known as "Cockroach Bogey". There are conflicting reports of how many soldiers this building was capable of feeding. Published reports tell that the building was capable of feeding 4000 soldiers at one time. A document written by a Major who was assigned to Jefferson Barracks during the 1940's indicates that the building could hold 1600 soldiers at one sitting. Either way you look at it, the building was extremely busy and filled to capacity during "chow" time. Atkinson Hall served as a focal point for soldiers stationed at Jefferson Barracks until the post's closing in 1946.

Building 78, or Atkinson Hall, as it looked in its heyday. For many years, this was one of the busiest buildings on the Post.

Many years after the post's closing, the Reserve and the National Guard renovated Building 78 for future occupation. During this restoration, a secret room was located on the third floor near the main stairway. Building plans that showed where walls had been constructed years after the Dining Facility was built, contradicted what the carpenters were seeing first hand. As a result, the suspicious wall was demolished. Inside, carpenters found a secluded room that contained military personal files, books, and pictures from a bygone era. This mystery is compounded by the rumor that the contractor who built the building in 1912, also committed suicide there years later.

Today, Building 78 is home to several units from the Missouri National Guard: Battery A, 128th Field Artillery, Detachment 1, 1137th Military Police, and the 1035th Maintenance Company. The building also seems to house its fair share of residual and interactive ghostly phenomena.

Several military and civilian employees on post have reported that the ghost of a WWI vet frequently returns to Building 78 to check on the building as if to insure that everything is alright. But this snippet of a story is just the tip of the iceberg when it comes to Atkinson Hall.

Atkinson Hall as it looks today

Major William "Willie" Smith, recounted a personal experience he had in Building 78 when he was the Battalion Logistics Officer assigned to the 1138th Engineer Battalion. Building 78 had been the previous home of the 1138th Engineer Battalion, prior to the unit's move to Building 27 in the early 1990's.

Major Smith had been working in the basement of the building by himself after hours. While walking down the basement hallway, on his way to the restroom, Major Smith suddenly felt like some unknown, unseen person was watching him walk down the hall. The feeling quickly passed, and Major Smith dismissed his apprehension, attributing it to the general "creepy atmosphere" of the building after hours. Continuing down the hallway towards the restroom which was just around a corner, Major Smith observed a "shadowy transparent form" cross the hallway in front of him.

"It was like catching a quick glimpse of something or someone moving in your peripheral vision," reported Major Smith. According to Major Smith, "the presence of this transparent shadow startled me because I was sure that I was the only person in the building at the time." But Major Smith's encounter was not over just yet.

Continuing down the hallway towards the intersection where just moments before, he had observed a shadow flit across his field of view, Major Smith got the shock of his life.

Just as he was about to walk around the corner into the intersecting hallway Major Smith observed the "shadowy form" peer around the corner at him. The transparent form lingered for a split second watching Major Smith's approach and then faded into thin air. When the shadow "just disappeared", Major Smith said that he was justifiably scared. "I turned on all of the lights that I could find in an attempt to see if anyone else was in the basement. It was different, it was like someone was really there."

Sergeant McWilliams, the same person who encountered the Confederate general at Building 1 earlier in this chapter, also recounted an experience he had in Building 78. When Sergeant McWilliams and another guardsman first started with the Funeral Honors Program, they lived in Building 78 for a short period of time. Sergeant McWilliams described several instances during the night and early morning, when he and his friend would feel "vibes" as if someone were in the building with them or watching them.

Sergeant McWilliams described how he and his friend would wake up at night and hear an unknown, unseen person walking up and down the stairs inside the building. McWilliams even reported how he experienced "hot spots" in various parts of the building, even when the air conditioning was working normally. In one particular instance, Sergeant McWilliams said that he woke up and the room in which he was sleeping was "icy cold, so cold you could see your breath" and moments later the room was warm again. After these varied encounters, Sergeant McWilliams is probably glad he lives off-post these days.

BUILDING 25

Building 25 was built in 1894 as enlisted soldiers quarters. Built much in the same style as Building's 28 and 29, this large rectangular building was used to billet enlisted soldiers and NCO's. At one time, the 1138th Military Police Battalion used the building as for administrative offices. Today, the building stands vacant, except for its "residual" occupants.

Steve Fonod, a retired guardsman, who currently works as a Distribution Manager for the Defense Energy Support Center in Building 66, remembers an incident that occurred in Building 25 when he was still assigned to the 1138th Military Police Battalion. One night, shortly after returning home, Mr. Fonod received a strange phone call from the security office at Jefferson Barracks.

The security officer wanted to inform Mr. Fonod that there were several lights left on in Building 25, and he was wondering if anyone was supposed to be working in the building after hours? The call concerned Mr. Fonod because he had turned out all of the lights and made sure that the building was secure prior to going home for the evening. Upon his arrival back at Building 25, Mr. Fonod found that lights had in fact been mysteriously turned back on in both the basement area and the first floor.

BUILDING 66

This three-story building, constructed in 1896, originally housed members of the 6th Infantry Army Band. After the post was decommissioned in 1946, guardsmen used the building for temporary quarters and later it would be used as overnight lodging exclusively for female soldiers. Civilian employees of the Defense Energy Support Center occupy Building 66 today.

Soldiers who have spent the night in Building 66 over the years, have reported hearing the terror-filled screams of women, children, and even babies during the night.

Several civilian employees working in the building after-hours have reported a myriad of unexplained events, which range from mysterious footsteps to noises in the attic. Residual paranormal activity is such an accepted part of the "office environment" for the civilian employees working in Building 66, that an employee posted a sign on the stairway leading to the third floor attic which states, "Resident Ghost Quarters, Do not Disturb".

Steve Fonod, the retired guardsman you met in the section regarding Building 25, said that he has personally heard strange banging noises emanating from the third-floor attic, doors opening and closing by themselves, and the sound of someone "shuffling" papers in a co-workers cubicle on the second floor. In each instance, Mr. Fonod was sure that he was the only one working in the building.

When Donna Schniederheins, a Budget Analyst working at the Defense Energy Support Center, first started working in Building 66, she had heard about the building's ghosts from other employees. In February 1999, Ms. Schniederheins was responsible for planning an important conference that was being held off-post. One evening during the conference, Ms. Schniederheins had to return to Building 66 to pick-up some equipment from the basement that was needed the next morning.

While in the basement, Ms. Schniederheins heard something "big" fall somewhere in the building. According to Ms. Schniederheins, "The basement walls of the supply room are pretty thick. After hearing that loud noise, I just flew out of the building."

Another weekend, while Ms. Schniederheins was working in the building by herself, she heard chairs and other furniture moving around on the second floor of the building. "It sounded like someone else was upstairs when I knew I was the only person in the building."

In another instance, Ms. Schniederheins had gone to the security office to see if someone else had keys to Building 66. Schniederheins and several of her co-workers were concerned because over a several week period, someone or something was turning on printers and computers after she and the other employees had turned them off the night before.

Security informed Ms. Schniederheins that they conduct nightly patrols of the area and that no one had been going into Building 66 after hours. In the same breath, the officer also told Ms. Schniederheins that a lot of strange things occur both on post and in Building 66 at night. The officer even hinted to the fact that there were some officers that would not go into certain buildings at night because of the strange things they have encountered through the years.

Ms. Schniederheins' suspicions about the presence of spirit energy in Building 66 would be confirmed by an unlikely source, her former boss's wife. The former department director's wife frequently visited Ms. Schniederheins and other employees working in the building. Schniederheins described this woman as being very intelligent, very well read on a variety of subjects, and very eccentric. Professing to have the ability to speak with the spirits in the building, the director's wife would frequently meditate up in the third-floor attic. One time, after returning from the attic, the former director's wife told Ms. Schniederheins not to worry because the ghosts that inhabited the building would not harm her.

When the former director's wife came to the office, she would sometimes bring her pet cat with her. Ms. Schniederheins said the cat often wandered around the office but that it would never go upstairs to the attic. According to Ms. Schniederheins, it was the actions of the cat that convinced her that there had to be some truth to what the director's wife had said about the ghosts.

Staff Sergeant Glenn McFarland, a training NCO serving with the 1138th Engineer Battalion, also encountered something "unseen" while living in Building 66 over a six-month period.

Staff Sergeant McFarland said that he frequently woke up at night and heard someone enter the building and go into one of the offices on the first floor. Each time, McFarland said that he got up and investigated the source of the strange noises but each time, he would find that he was the only person present in the building. Other nights, the sound of drawers opening and closing or the ghostly sounds of something cooking in the kitchen disturbed Staff Sergeant McFarland's slumber. On these nights, when McFarland went to the kitchen to ascertain the who or what could be clanging pots and pans together, he found the kitchen lights on. Each time this occurred, Staff Sergeant McFarland was sure that he had turned off all the lights in the building prior to going to bed.

He even experienced these strange events during the day. He described how small items would be knocked off desks, and how a picture hanging on the wall in the squad bay would become "drastically tilted" when you were not looking.

Staff Sergeant McFarland believes that the unseen 'spirits' he feels he has encountered while working at Jefferson Barracks, are practical jokers and that they are definitely not malevolent. McFarland describes the actions of these pesky poltergeists as being similar to those of children or that of a practical joker. Staff Sergeant McFarland stated, "things are always missing or moved when you need them. You look for something you know was just there and then two, three days later, the item you needed two days earlier, is right there where you looked for it the first time."

Having also spent his fair share of time in building 78, Staff Sergeant McFarland thinks that every building at Jefferson Barracks has a resident ghost living in it. " I could swear that there have been times that I have been working alone in this building or that on post, and that I have heard someone, or something, else moving around in the building."

BUILDING 27 & 27A

Located almost exactly at the opposite end (west) of post, from Building 1, stands Building 27. Building 27 was built in 1896 as enlisted soldiers quarters. This large rectangular building has a three-story center and two story wings jutting out to each side that could hold up to four companies of soldiers and NCO's. The original mess hall for the building was located in the basement, but in the early 1940's, a smaller one-story building, Building 27A, was built directly behind Building 27 and was used as a mess hall. Today, Building 27 is the home of the 1138th Engineer Battalion, and Building 27A serves as the administrative area for the battalion's Headquarters Detachment.

Both buildings play host to phantoms that are residual and interactive in nature. One veteran battalion supply sergeant commented that he was always looking for a light switch to turn on when he was working in the building alone because he sometimes felt "apprehensive" or like "some one was watching him". A battalion staff officer. who frequently spends the night in Building 27, said that on at least one occasion, he thought he heard "muffled footsteps" and doors opening and closing by themselves when no one else was present in the building.

Security Officer Dickson, whom you have already met, told me during my interview with him, "that everywhere you go on this post, you feel like someone is watching you". This was apparently the case one evening when Officer Dickson was working the Midnight Shift. He was sitting in the old "Guard Shack" next to Building 27, when he observed a 6' human form duck behind the building. As Officer Dickson had just completed a complete check of the area, and was sure that no one was working in the building at the time, he went to investigate the situation further.

Dickson exited his cozy "guard shack" and proceeded to the other end of the building in an attempt to cut the unidentified "form" off at the pass, so to speak. When he got to the far end of the building, he waited, and waited, and waited. Officer Dickson could hear someone or something walking through the dead leaves that had accumulated between the buildings but no one ever passed him. After waiting for what seemed like an eternity, the intrepid security officer decided that he would check the doors in between the buildings and found each one secured. The phantom had vanished without a trace.

In September 2000, Specialist Nicole Howell, a Personnel Clerk for the 235th Engineer Company, got the shock of her life when she observed the phantom of a "Calvary Scout" in the main foyer of Building 27. Specialist Howell described the male Civil War-era soldier as wearing striped uniform riding pants, a sword and shoulder-length brown hair. When Specialist Howell first saw the figure, she could see the boots and pants walking around the foyer and then she could see the soldier's upper torso and hair. As the figment moved about the foyer, it appeared to "phase" in and out. She first saw the boots and pants walking and moving around the foyer, and then she observed the soldier's upper torso and hair materialize right before her eyes.

Howell said that she later observed the same "Scout" on the landing stairs leading to the second floor of the building, and a third time in the building's mailroom. Each time Specialist Howell described the phantom, she reiterated that the soldier appeared to be translucent and phase in and out. According to Specialist Howell she feels that the "Calvary Scout" fancies himself a "lady's man" and will only appear or make himself known when female soldiers are present in the building.

(Right) The staircase landing where Specialist Howell reportedly saw the ghost of the "Scout"

Howell told me that she has frequently felt like "someone" is watching her when there is no one else present in the building. She also stated that she had a really unusual experience in July 2000... as if seeing the transparent figure of a civil war Calvary scout would not be unusual enough.

Specialist Howell said that she became a little "unnerved" when her standard electric typewriter suddenly came to life as if it had a mind of its own and started to "return" by itself. As Howell watched in amazement, the typewriter continued to function by itself for several seconds.

But Specialist Howell is not the only member of the Howell family who has experienced something supernatural in Building 27.

Specialist Howell's husband, Sergeant Charles Howell, Administrative NCO for the 203rd Engineer Company, also had several "unnerving" encounters in both Building 27 and 27A. The strange events started to unfold in April 2000, when Sergeant Howell was working by himself in the building. During the early morning or early evening hours, Sergeant Howell started to get the feeling that someone or "something" was watching him and even in some cases following him around the building.

According to the Sergeant, this unseen energy "made the hair on the back of my neck stand up" and that he would get "weird vibes all afternoon, and just know something would happen".

"You will be sitting there working, and all of a sudden you will get the creeps and think to yourself, what the hell was that?" Sergeant Howell estimated that a lot of strange things seemed to happen in the early morning hours or between 4pm and 7pm. "You know that you are not alone, and yet you know you are the only one working in the building".

Sergeant Howell suggested that the second floor "command" area, to include the office used by the Battalion's commander, is the most unsettling area of the building. One time, Sergeant Howell said he had work to do on the second floor, and he felt like "he was interrupting the ghosts or that they did not want him there". When this happened, Sergeant Howell stated out loud, "I have work to do, and I have every right to be up here working." In addition to the second floor of the building, Sergeant Howell also indicated that he believes that the Mailroom in Building 27 is extremely active with paranormal energy.

On a cold morning in April 2000, Sergeant Howell had another encounter with one of the spirits in Building 27. On this particular morning, Sergeant Howell was working by himself in the unit's old supply closet, located in the basement of Building 27.

While Sergeant Howell was busy counting equipment he again felt that "someone" was watching him. Sergeant Howell continued to count various items, and a short time later, he thought he saw a brown boot out of the corner of his eye. Thinking that someone was standing in the room watching him, he turned to see who it was, but immediately observed that no one was in the room with him and that the boot was gone. Now, really feeling uneasy, Sergeant Howell decided that he was going to leave. When he turned off the lights inside the room and started to walk out the door into the hallway, the lights suddenly turned back on again. By this time, Sergeant Howell was becoming frustrated and said," knock this @*$& off. I don't have time for your @#$^". Sergeant Howell never did tell me if he stuck around to see if the ghosts replied.

Sergeant Howell later reported other experiences with lights turning on and off by themselves. This time, he was in the Annex, Building 27A. Sergeant Howell was going home for the evening and after turning off the light, had locked the heavy wooden door separating the annex and the main building. He observed that the lights were turned back on. When Sergeant Howell unlocked the door and looked at the light switch, he found that indeed, someone or something had turned on the lights at the switch.

On another occasion, Sergeant Howell was leaving after locking the Annex, and the lights mysteriously turned on by themselves again. When he unlocked the door, and turned the lights off again, the lights turned back on while he was re-locking the door.

But the best was yet to come.

In March 2001, Sergeant Howell was again working late in Building 27A, going through administration files in the Orderly Room, located just inside the Annex. Sergeant Howell again got the feeling, or "impression", that someone was watching him. When Sergeant Howell looked up, he observed a man in the office leaning toward him. The visitor was husky in build and was wearing a blue, Spanish American War uniform shirt, khaki pants, and a cowboy-style hat of that time period. Because of the way this ghostly visitor was dressed, Sergeant Howell was struck by the thought that this soldier looked as if he could have been with Teddy Roosevelt and the "Rough Riders" during their famous charge up San Juan Hill. Sergeant Howell remarked that he thought that the soldier was probably "enlisted" because he did not see any officer rank or stripes on the soldier's shirt or collar.

Sergeant Howell looked back down at his files not really realizing the significance of the moment, and immediately, he did a double-take and looked back at the soldier. Just as he looked up, he observed the phantom fade away. Sergeant Howell knew immediately that he had finally identified his prankster.

In April 2001, Sergeant Howell experienced another "creepy" encounter with this "Prankster" when he was again working late in the Orderly Room. Sergeant Howell had locked the hallway door and had turned off the hallway lights. He had left the door to the Orderly Room open and was working quietly, when all of a sudden, he heard the hallway door "slam" open, and then he heard heavy footsteps walking down the hall towards his office.

Sergeant Howell knew he had locked the hallway door and so he got up to see if anyone was there. While he was making his way toward the doorway, Howell heard the heavy footsteps approach his office. He waited to see if he could see anyone walk by his office but instead, the ghostly footsteps continued past his office and down to the end of the hall. Sergeant Howell never observed what made the sounds but he guessed that it was the soldier he had seen previously in the office. After collecting his wits, Sergeant Howell checked the heavy hallway door, and found it locked. Realizing that he still had work to do, Sergeant Howell closed his office door and turned up the volume on his radio so he would not hear any more noises in the hall.

In early 2001, Sergeant Howell had an unusual encounter with a living visitor. Sergeant Howell was working in the building, and had the opportunity to meet an elderly World War II veteran who stopped by the building "just to take a look around". Sergeant Howell learned that the man had been a member of the 1st Battalion, 6th Infantry Division when it had been stationed at Jefferson Barracks in the late 1930's. The 6th Infantry Division would later fight in Africa during the World War II, with General George S. Patton.

The old battle-hardened veteran told Sergeant Howell where each of the units of the battalion were housed in Building 27. Each wing of the first floor and the second floor were open "bays". Each wing housed a company of enlisted soldiers. The central core of the building was used to billet unit NCO's. The basement of the building was used for storage and food preparation/ mess operations.

The basement was so large, that it also served as an indoor weapons range. The third floor of the building was used as a recreation room where the soldiers could play pool, cards, or just listen to music.

The veteran even let Sergeant Howell in on several forgotten secrets, like the little known exits and entrances where the soldiers would sneak out to meet clandestinely with a sweetheart or where sometimes the sweetheart was spirited inside the building for a meeting closer to home.

Sergeant Howell even learned that cramped damp storage space under the basement stairs once housed one of the company commander's black orderlies This mystery visitor also told Sergeant Howell that even as long ago as the 1930's, soldiers heard strange noises in the building and that some of them were even "spooked" by what they experienced.

During the course of my interview with Sergeant Howell, he gave me some insight into his life when he was younger. Prior to living in Missouri, Sergeant Howell encountered what he believed to be an evil spirit in California. Based on this previous encounter with the unknown, Sergeant Howell believes that there are several ghosts that inhabit Building 27 and that each one is really harmless and would not hurt anyone.

Sergeant Howell feels that the building is "overflowing" with spirit energy and surmised that the increased amount of paranormal activity could be caused by the lead paint that is still on walls in parts of the building. "I know that lead was used in the early photographic and tape recording processes. This dense material could be a key to what is going on." Sergeant Howell concluded the interview with a very sobering yet sensitive statement," These are the spirits of old soldiers. They had a job to do, and they recognize us as being soldiers, and they know we have jobs to do."

Building 27 has two more ghost stories to tell. This tale comes from Corporal Melissa Squires, another female soldier who worked in Building 27 for several years prior to being transferred to another unit. Almost from the time she started working in Building 27, Corporal Squires began to "hear things". When she would mention her observations to other employees working in the building, they told her that it was just her imagination.

In October 1999, Corporal Squires was working late in the building by herself. As she continued to work into the night, Corporal Squires started to hear someone walking around on the second floor of the building in the squad bay right over her head. This occurred several times during the next couple of nights. Each time, Corporal Squires checked the building and the front parking lot. Every time, she found that no one else had come into the building after it was locked for the night.

By March 2000, Corporal Squires started to hear noises and banging sounds emanating from the basement below her work area. Squires described the noises as being similar to someone banging on the basement floor with a broom. Later, Corporal Squires started to hear unexplained "thumps" and "bumps" on the walls of the building. Again, Corporal Squires mentioned the odd noises to her fellow co-workers, and again she was told that she was crazy and that the noises were the product of her imagination.

Several months later, Corporal Squires got the scare of her life. Just like before, she was working in Building 27 after hours, and again, she heard muffled footsteps on the second floor of the building. Summoning all of her courage, she went up to the second floor to see what was responsible for making these eerie noises. When Corporal Squires reached the hallway on the second floor, in front of the Battalion Commander's office, she suddenly was awash in intense heat.

"I started to get goose bumps and I immediately turned around and started to walk back down the steps" remarked Corporal Squires. When she reached the main foyer, she collected her wits and returned to her office to work on some more paperwork. A short time later, Corporal Squires heard the footsteps again, only this time, as she listened, she noticed that they were walking down the stairs to the main foyer.

Squires did not wait around to see who or what was walking down the steps. Instead, she immediately vacated the building at a high rate of speed, leaving her purse and other personal valuables on her desk. "They told me that it was an old building... but I know footsteps when I hear them."

MY OWN EXPERIENCES IN BUILDING 27A

This book would not be complete if I did not mention my own personal experience in Building 27A. I was working late one evening on some paperwork. The unit was preparing to go to Annual Training and a small contingent of soldiers from my unit were scheduled to leave early the next morning.

One soldier who was set to depart had come to the unit the day before because he lived quite a distance from the armory and did not want to drive there early in the morning. I knew the soldier might be staying in the building and was aware that the soldier had spent the night there on many other occasions.

As the night wore on, I started to hear someone moving around on the second floor of the building. I did not really give it any thought at the time because I thought it was this same soldier getting ready to bed down for the evening. The rest of the night, I would periodically hear thumps and bumps of someone going about their business in the building.

When I had finally concluded my business for the evening, I paged the soldier that I thought was staying in the building. I requested that he meet me in the front foyer so I could find out what doors needed to be locked for the night. I no more than hung the phone up when I heard someone come running down the stairs from the second floor. I then heard the person come through the main foyer, enter the Annex, and suddenly come to a stop outside of my office door.

I was packing my suitcase, and thinking that the person standing outside of my office was the soldier I had paged, I commented out loud that he did not have to wait outside my office while I finished packing. I asked the soldier to come into my office several times, and when no one came in, I started to get concerned. What made matters worse, was the fact that I was sure that someone had to be in the hallway because I never heard anyone leave the area. After waiting for a few more seconds, I looked out into the hall.

No one was there.

I paged the soldier again over the intercom and again requested that he meet me in the front lobby. I went to the lobby and waited for five minutes or more. No one ever arrived. I knew that someone was in the building, but I did not know where. First I checked the basement, thinking that the soldier could have gone there to pack some equipment for his trip. When I did not find the soldier there, I searched the rest of the building, floor by floor. Needless to say, I was the only person in the building.

By now, I was getting a little "spooked" myself. I had been doing research for this book for some time, and I was aware of the ghost stories in the building. Taking this into account, I did not want to blow the situation out of proportion.

The next morning, I met with the soldier who I thought was in the building the night before. He told me that as soon as he had been dismissed for the day, he changed his clothes and had gone to his sister-in-law's house. The soldier said that at no time had he returned to the building the previous night, and that about the time I heard someone run down the stairs and stop outside my office, he was eating dinner at a local restaurant.

I have been investigating haunted houses for many years and because I have a law enforcement background, I am more than a bit skeptical about things. On this particular night, I know for a fact that someone was moving around the building and that someone or something responded to my page.

For me, my experience in Building 27A proved without a shadow of a doubt that there had to be some truth to the ghost stories I had collected from the civilians and soldiers working at Jefferson Barracks.

CHAPTER SIX

OFF-POST HAUNTS

One could not write a book about the legends of Jefferson Barracks without taking into account the other various haunted locations that fall outside of the current military reservation. The one hundred and thirty five acres that comprise the core of Jefferson Barracks today is just a small portion of the post's original 1700 acres.

The remaining buildings and property, which were deemed "surplus" by the United States government in 1946, now belong to private and public entities. Yet many of these locations are still haunted today by their historical past. As in the previous chapter, the following stories and encounters have been grouped under the building or site where they allegedly occurred.

THE POWDER MAGAZINE

Built in 1857, this massive limestone building, enclosed by a rectangular stone wall, was used to store munitions. Rifles, cannons and gunpowder were stored at this location for later use by the troops stationed at Jefferson Barracks. In 1871, the Federal Arsenal in St. Louis was closed and its contents were moved to Jefferson Barracks for storage. The Powder Magazine was a storage facility up until the military reservation was closed in 1946. Today, the building is a museum maintained by the St. Louis County Parks and Recreation Department, and it is one of the favorite attractions of the Jefferson Barracks Historic Park.

Jefferson Barrack's old Powder Magazine, where the ghost of a Civil War era sentry is rumored to still patrol.

One of the early legends documented for posterity by author Tony Fusco in his compilation of articles titled *Historic Jefferson Barracks*, involves the Powder Magazine. When America was thrust into the Second World War by the Japanese attack on Pearl Harbor on December 7, 1941, armed soldiers at Jefferson Barracks were deployed at key positions around the post. One of these important locations, was the Powder Magazine. Armed sentries were frequently seen walking along the top of the stone wall surrounding the magazine or they would be observed patrolling around the exterior of the building.

Several of the soldiers who had pulled "guard mount" at the Powder Magazine, reported seeing a ghostly sentry who would appear every so often and challenge a bewildered guard at his post. It was believed that the ghost was the spirit of a murdered sentry who had been killed by a raiding party while they were trying to steal munitions from the Powder Magazine. This unsettled spirit, described as "having a bullet hole in his head, running red with blood" is said to have accosted his living counterparts because in death, he had been deprived of fulfilling his rightful duty.

An encounter with this ghost was said to be such a frightful experience that several guards reportedly threw down their weapons and deserted their posts after seeing this shade. In one extreme instance, a soldier not only left his guard post, but also left the army as well because of his encounter with this unearthly sentry.

When I spoke to Mr. Fusco about this story, he said that it had no real basis in fact. According to his research, there had been no armed incursions onto the post that would explain the soldier's death. Mr. Fusco did say that during the Civil War, Confederate soldiers conducted a reconnaissance of the Powder Magazine from an island that was located in the Mississippi River across from the post. It is said that these would-be attackers paddled to the island and acted as if they were having a picnic while they secretly noted the Federal Defenses. Federal officers at Jefferson Barracks ordered extra troops into the area, and the Confederate picnicker's decided it was in their best interest not to attack the post.

THE OLD NORTH GATE

A second ghostly tale, chronicled by Mr. Fusco, involves a supernatural phantom that is said to haunt the grounds near the old north gate. The transparent ghost of 2nd Lieutenant Thomas O. May is alleged to return from the pale on the anniversary of his death, searching for his soul near the place "where he had been dispatched from his earthly entanglements by the sword". 2nd Lt. Thomas O. May, a young officer in his 20's from Vermont, was killed in a duel near the Old North Gate in1830. To this day, Mr. Fusco has been unable to determine exactly how 2nd Lt. May was killed.

THE LABORER'S HOUSE

This building, which is supposed to be haunted by the ghost of an unidentified woman, was constructed in 1851. Civilians working at the Ordnance Depot primarily used this building as a residence. During the

1950's an extensive archeological survey was done at the same location where the restored building stands today. The building is part of the Jefferson Barracks Historic Park and is used as a "Gift Shop". The garden at the rear of the building is frequently reserved for outdoor weddings, teas, and other special events.

VETERANS ADMINISTRATION MEDICAL CENTER

Ever since the foundation of Jefferson Barracks in 1826, the post had maintained some form of hospital facilities for the treatment of its troops. During the Civil War, Jefferson Barracks would prove to be the most influential military medical complex in the United States.

On January 9, 1922, President Warren G. Harding would transfer 170 acres of the military reservation, south of the National Cemetery, for the construction of a Veterans Hospital. This new hospital, completed in March 1923, was tasked with the treatments of wounded and invalid soldiers, and has provided continuous medical service to military veterans ever since it opened it doors.

Three separate variations of one ghost story involve the Veterans Hospital. A Security Supervisor relayed a story that he had heard about an incident that was supposed to have occurred at the hospital. One Halloween night there was a private costume party held at the hospital. After the event, security officers working the main gate at the hospital commented to one of the party's organizers about the "excellent" Civil War costume one of the guests had worn to the party. The party organizer told the security officer that no one in attendance at the party had been wearing a costume of that type. This apparently caused the officer some concern because he distinctly remembered allowing a man wearing a Civil War era costume enter the hospital grounds presumably to attend the party because of the way he was dressed.

In the second version, a man dressed as a Civil War soldier was said to be standing guard outside of the building where the Halloween party was held. The courteous guard greeted the arriving guests and allowed them to enter the building.

In the last version of this story, a small "private" costume party was being held at the hospital during Halloween. The host of the party, an unnamed employee of the hospital, observed a man dressed in a Civil War-era costume, sitting on a stone wall amidst the other costumed guests. The host approached the man and asked him how he liked the party so far. The soldiers comment, "Liked it good" was barely a whisper. The host, apparently taken aback by the guest's crude response, started to walk away. When the host turned around seconds later, the guest in the Civil War costume was gone. It was later determined that no one invited to the party or in attendance at the event on the evening in question, was wearing a Civil War costume.

JEFFERSON BARRACKS "STATION" HOSPITAL

The Jefferson Barracks "Station" Hospital was built around 1905. It would serve the soldiers and families assigned to post until the Military Reservation was closed in 1946. The third floor of this large brick, three-story building was used for surgery suites and the basement of the building housed the morgue.

When the hospital was closed in 1946, it became the property of the Mehlville School District. The school used the vacated building as a high school for several years and today, the building is used for the school district's Facility Department.

School district employees who have worked in the building after hours report hearing ghostly footsteps at various locations inside the building and also several incidents where the building's lights have been mysteriously turned on and off. In addition to these paranormal phenomena, the ghost of a little girl has been observed in the basement by at least one employee.

One employee told me about her experience in the building's old morgue. This particular female employee has worked in the building for four years. She said that in the time she has been working in the building, she has only been in the old morgue once. "When I left the morgue, I know that something I could not see came out with me."

I had an opportunity to tour the third floor of the old hospital and see the morgue first-hand. The third floor of the building is now vacant but the morgue is still used as a storage area. The morgue itself is broken down into separate rooms. A heavy metal door separates each room from the morgue's main hallway. When I entered the morgue, I immediately noticed a sudden temperature drop. This sudden change in temperature caused goose bumps to breakout on my arms and for a split second I felt like I just wanted to leave the area as soon as possible. These feelings passed and I continued my tour, taking several pictures along the way.

(Right) The door to the creepy morgue area of the basement

I cannot say that what I experienced on that particular occasion was anything supernatural. Being the skeptic that I am, I attribute the sudden temperature drop to the solid stone construction of the building and the morgue itself. The morgue had to function for several years without the luxury of air conditioning, so it was naturally built to be the coolest place in the building. I believe the atmosphere of the morgue itself was so overwhelming initially, that it was my natural instinct to want to leave, or was that all it was?

BUILDING 96

Even though this building is outside of the boundaries of the current National Guard base, Building 96 is still maintained by the military. Built in 1942 by, and for, the American Red Cross, this building has served as soldier billets, an Army and Air National Guard recruiting station, and as a Coast Guard post-exchange. Today, the building houses the administrative offices for the Funeral Honors Programs.

When Building 96 was used as a barracks for soldiers, it was nicknamed "Harry's Hilton" in honor of the 80 year-old retired guardsman who maintained the building. One half of the building was set aside for female soldiers and the other half was sectioned off for male soldiers. "Harry" the caretaker also lived in the building and did his best to serve the needs of the soldiers who paid $2.00 dollars a night to stay there. No one seems to know what happened to "Harry" after the building was converted in a recruiting station in 1987.

Sergeant First Class Donald Wisdom was assigned to Building 96 as an Army National Guard recruiter in 1996, when the building was still being used as a recruiting station.

Wisdom's office was located at the end of the south wing of the building. As part of his job as a recruiter, he was frequently required to work late into the evening in order to process possible new recruits. When he would work late, he would insure that all of the entrances and exits to the building were locked. This included the large heavy door, which served as the building's main entrance.

Sergeant First Class Wisdom reported that on many of the occasions when he was working late by himself, he would hear someone open the front door of the building, then he would hear footsteps in the hallway. Each time this occurred, Wisdom said that he checked all of the building's interior offices and every door leading in and out of the building. Every time, Sergeant First Class Wisdom determined without a doubt that he was the only person in the building and that every door was locked.

In 1985, Master Sergeant Don Allen, a Personnel Superintendent for the Air National Guard who also worked as a recruiter with Sergeant First Class Wisdom at the time, reported having a ghostly encounter of his own in Building 96. On this particular night in question, Allen was working in the building by himself. He was waiting in his office, located immediately to right of the foyer and main entrance to the building, for the arrival of a possible new enlistee.

As the time neared for the prospective new soldier to arrive, Master Sergeant Allen heard the unmistakable "click" of someone opening the heavy metal door at the main entrance to the building, and then the sound of the door slamming shut. Almost immediately, he heard someone walking along the tile floor of the building's main hallway. Thinking that some unauthorized person, or that his prospective soldier, may have entered the building, Master Sergeant Allen checked the front door and foyer. No one was in the lobby. He confirmed that no one else was in the building and then returned to his office dumbfounded by who or what had opened the door of the building.

A short time later, the new soldier arrived for his meeting. During this meeting, Master Sergeant Allen told the new soldier about what had happened just prior to his arrival. After considering what had just transpired, both Master Sergeant Allen and the new enlistee decided to cut the meeting short on that particular evening.

Several months later, Allen was meeting with other recruiters who worked in Building 96. During this meeting, a fellow Army National Guard recruiter told Allen that he used to spend the night in the building and that on several occasions, he also heard the main door of the building mysteriously open and close for no apparent reason

The unnamed Army recruiter also reported that in each instance, the sound of the door opening and closing was always accompanied by ghostly footsteps. The Army recruiter confided in Master Sergeant Allen and told him that because of these unexplained noises, he no longer slept in the building.

Could "Harry" still be keeping track of the building he maintained for so many years? It would appear that anything is possible at Jefferson Barracks.

JEFFERSON BARRACKS NATIONAL CEMETERY

The Jefferson Barracks National Cemetery is an extension of the Old Post Cemetery that was established in 1827. When the National Cemetery came into existence in 1866, it became a place where the remains of modern day heroes would be intermingled with the military and civilian dead of a former frontier post that guarded the gateway to the west during a tumultuous time in America's history.

As you learned in a previous chapter, which outlined the history of the National Cemetery, Elizabeth Ann Lash, the daughter of an army officer stationed at Jefferson Barracks, was laid to rest in the Old Post Cemetery, on August 5, 1827.

Employees of the cemetery and at least one soldier assigned to Jefferson Barracks have reported that the ghost of Elizabeth Lash has been observed walking between the white marble gravestones near her final place of rest.

During my interview with Specialist Howell, she mentioned that she had heard stories about the ghost of a little girl wandering around the Jefferson Barracks National Cemetery. Howell admitted that she had heard this information "second hand" and that it was hard to tell exactly where the girl's ghost was really observed because so many of the old buildings have been torn down over the years.

The grave of Elizabeth Lash is located on a peaceful hillside overlooking the Mississippi River, Old Post Section 1, grave 2229- A. Her marble tombstone, inlayed with the traditional union shield, is nondescript and does not bare any indications of its significance to the cemetery.

Absent from the headstone are kind passing words from Elizabeth's grieving parents, now long dead and buried. But is what is being reported as the ghost of a small child, really the remnant of Elizabeth Lash? My research into the history of the cemetery indicates that there could be another explanation for this toddler-like manifestation.

Shortly after Superintendent Past started working at the National Cemetery in 1900, he unearthed the remains of several unidentified children whose graves had been obscured by bushes and undergrowth in the Old Post section of the cemetery. As in the case of Elizabeth Lash, the identities and causes of death of these children will never be known. What is known, is that a great cholera epidemic swept through the Mississippi Valley in 1830. Possibly this disease, or some other calamity of the frontier, caused the children's early demise. The children were listed as "unknown" and buried in individual gravesites.

The melancholy grave marker of Elizabeth Lash in the National Cemetery

For whatever reason, it is entirely possible that one these little "unknown's" is actually roaming the oldest part of the cemetery, not Elizabeth Lash. Why? We may never really know. Maybe this is a little boy or girl's last chance to make extra-sensory contact with just the right person who could possibly put a name with a face, so that these long dead and buried souls can finally be recognized.

THE GHOSTS OF THE NORTH AND SOUTH MAKE THEIR PEACE

When I interviewed Major Willie Smith in regards to his personal experiences in Building 78, we happened upon the topic of ghostly occurrences in the National Cemetery. Major Smith smiled and stated that he had heard from unnamed cemetery employees, that a section of the Jefferson Barracks National Cemetery is haunted by the specter-like forms of a Civil War, Union "Buffalo Soldier" and a Civil War Confederate soldier.

At this unknown location, Black Union soldiers, also known as "Buffalo" soldiers, and Confederate soldiers are buried in close proximity to each other. Major Smith said that he had been told that this ghostly union is best observed during the early evening hours, around dusk and during the early morning hours, around dawn. It has been said the shadows of these two long dead adversaries can be seen floating in between the Confederate graves and the Union graves, as if moving towards each other.

When the shapeless forms finally get close to each other, they allegedly each extend an open hand as if greeting one another in friendship one last time. Major Smith hypothesized that that these valiant heroes of a bygone era are doomed to continuously try to make peace, not only for themselves but for their fallen comrades in arms.

Major Smith curiously noted that the Confederate gravestones in the cemetery are different from the Union graves because they have a pointed top. Major Smith said that he had heard that old Confederate soldiers used to joke that their graves had points on them so that no Union soldier would ever sit on the grave of a valiant Confederate soldier who had passed on into the next world.

AFTERWORD

Is Jefferson Barracks haunted by the spirits of its historic past?

You have read about the individual stories of sacrifice, glory, and heroism that have been the foundation of this frontier post's richness and diversity. You have also learned about just a few of the phantoms that appear to linger both on and off post to this day.

What do you think? Does the ghost of a Civil War Confederate general haunt the post commander's office in Building 1? Can the spirits of Black "Buffalo" soldiers and Confederate war dead buried at the Jefferson Barracks National Cemetery be seen by dawn's early light, reconciling a long over due "peace". Does the ghost of little Elizabeth Lash haunt the National Cemetery or is the manifestation observed in the Old Post Section of the cemetery, really the disembodied specters of the unidentified children who's graves were lost and then found 70 years later? I do not know the answers to these questions, but I know what I personally experienced in Building 27A was typical of an "intelligent" haunting.

Since there is no definitive proof that ghosts and phantoms even exist, I default to a quote from T.C. Lethbridge, a noted British archaeologist, who wrote *Ghost and Ghoul*, when questions like these arise.

"I must emphasize that one can only be one's own guinea pig in the matters of the supernatural. No spoken or written word can be a substitute for one's own practical experience. No one too can convince another who does not wish to believe what he or she is told. Only the doubter loses by his or her incredulity."

You probably recognize this passage from the list of quotes at the beginning of this book. For the last 10 years, I have frequently referred back to T.C. Lethbridge's immortal words of wisdom as I have attempted to unravel the paranormal mysteries that I have encountered at the various locations I have personally investigated. Only after experiencing an unexplained encounter with one of the "unknowns" at Jefferson Barracks, will you truly believe in the existence of ghosts.

Now I know what you are thinking. "How will I be able to go to Jefferson Barracks and possibly have a supernatural encounter of my own?" In the near future, this may be easier than you think.

The Missouri National Guard, in cooperation with the Museum Studies Program at the University of Missouri- St. Louis (UMSL), is developing an exciting concept in which a portion of the existing post would be turned into a museum aptly titled "Jefferson Barracks: a Celebration of the Citizen Soldier". The St. Louis County Parks and Recreation Department, the Jefferson Barracks National Cemetery, and the Veterans Hospital are also key parties in this truly collaborative effort.

This bold plan will preserve the 175-year heritage of Jefferson Barracks for future generations to come. Many of the existing period buildings described in this book, would be remodeled and incorporated into special interactive historical programs, military technology displays and even a visitor hospitality center and restaurant.

Visitors to the museum would be able to watch or participate in actual archaeological digs and see first-and what it takes to preserve artifacts already uncovered. In addition, hundreds of thousands of people visiting the site will have the opportunity to take walking tours of historical graves and locations in the National Cemetery or to take carriage and wagon rides through the park.

This is a purposed endeavor that is far from becoming a reality. I cannot say with any degree of certainty that this museum project will ever be completed during my lifetime. But if it does, be wary of the Civil War re-enactor dressed as the Confederate general you see while you are eating lunch at the museum restaurant, also known as Building 1.

The "old general" may or may not be who or what you think he is.

APPENDIX

THE LAYMAN'S CHRONOLOGY OF JEFFERSON BARRACKS AND THE ST. LOUIS REGION

In conducting the historical research for this book, I consulted countless printed works archived in various libraries, museums, and computer databases in the St. Louis area. Every new piece of factual information I uncovered in my pursuit of the past seemed to lead me down two or three new paths of inquiry. As anyone who knows what it is like to become totally immersed in a hobby or passion, I soon found myself surrounded by ever expanding piles of relevant electronic and hardbound information that was easy to loose track of. As I felt that my continued inquiries held various keys to important pieces of "behind the scenes" narration that helped to shape Jefferson Barracks over the last 175 years; I began to make a chronology of the information I unearthed.

I feel that the sheer number of individual trials, tribulations, and sacrifices experienced by the vast number of soldiers who lived and died at Jefferson Barracks over the years, serves as an impetus for most, if not all, of the ghostly encounters experienced there today. To that end, I wanted to provide the reader with an easy to understand chronology of particular events significant to the St. Louis region and Jefferson Barracks proper. Important people, places and events were selected due to their relevance to everyday life and death at the post.

After reading this chronology, you will see how the turbulent time period, with its technological advances in transportation, medicine, and the art of war, directly reflected upon the every day life of the infantryman in the field. Now I know that some learned critics in the audience will probably look at my timeline and say, "he forgot this or how could he have left out that". To them, I want to reiterate that the goal of this book was to capture the varied and unnerving experiences of the men and women stationed at Jefferson Barracks both in the past and present, while imparting a little local history and color along the way.

I will preface the following list of events with a cautionary note. In reviewing various historical sources, I noted that in some instances, a few dates were off by a year or two. When I encountered these rare deviations, I endeavored to use the most consistent dates reported by a majority of the sources I researched.

April 1764: The village of St. Louis is founded. It is named in honor of Louis IX, patron saint of France.

1767: The village of Carondelet was founded near the River de Peres.

1776: The American struggle for Independence begins.

1804: The Louisiana Purchase is completed and all of the land west of the Mississippi River fall under the control of the United States.

1805: Fort Bellefountaine established by the United States near the confluence of the Missouri and Mississippi Rivers.

August 10, 1821: Missouri becomes the 24th state in the union. Missouri is considered a "slave state" under the provisions of the Missouri Compromise.

July 8, 1826: The U.S. Government enters into a contract with the Village of Carondelet to purchase 1702 acres of land for the establishment of a new military post to replace Fort Bellefountaine. Asking price for the land, a gold coin equating to $5.00 dollars. At the time of this purchase, many felt that Fort Bellefountaine had been built in an unhealthy location and had fallen into a state of disrepair.

July 10, 1826: Four companies of the 1st Infantry Regiment under the command of Major Stephen Watts Kearny, arrived at the future site of Jefferson Barracks.

October, 23 1826: The new post is designated as the army's first "Infantry

School of Practice" and is aptly named "Jefferson Barracks" in honor of President Thomas Jefferson who died on July 4, 1826.

August 5, 1827: Elizabeth Ann Lash, the eighteen-month old daughter of an army officer stationed at Jefferson Barracks, is buried in the "Old Post Cemetery" over looking the Mississippi River, Old Post Section 1, grave 2229-A.

1829: Due to increased Indian problems between western Missouri and Santa Fe, the first armed contingents from Jefferson Barracks begin escorting merchants along the Santa Fe Trail.

1832: U.S. Army and Missouri Militia troops from Jefferson Barracks take part in the Fox and Sac Indian War. Chief Black Hawk and a band of about 1,000 Indians are defeated at the battle of Bad Axe River. Chief Black Hawk and several other warriors taken prisoner after the battle and are escorted to Jefferson Barracks by Lt. Jefferson Davis.

1835: Dr. William Beaumont arrives at Jefferson Barracks and begins his five year tour of service as the post's "Surgeon General". Though Beaumont is considered to be one of the six great heroes of "American Medical Science", on at least one occasion, in 1884, he is accused of medical malpractice.

1836: U.S. Army troops and Missouri Militia from Jefferson Barracks take part in the Seminole Indian War in Florida.

1841: The original post chronometer (sundial) was placed on the bluff overlooking the Mississippi River. The face of the sundial was later stolen. The original foundation of the chronometer, with a new sundial, is located behind Building 1.

1846-48: Congress declares war with Mexico. Jefferson Barracks serves as "stepping off point" for military units participating in the war.

1849-50: The city of St. Louis and surrounding areas, to include Jefferson

Barracks, experiences an Asiatic cholera epidemic. As a result of the epidemic, Chouteau Pond was drained. Also around this time, the St. Louis Boat landing is heavily damaged by fire. This disastrous fire destroyed 15 city blocks along the river front and engulfed 23 steamboat moored along the landing.

1851: The above ground Ordnance Room, Laborer's House and Stables are constructed at the north end of Jefferson Barracks. These stone structures are still being used today and are maintained by the St. Louis County Parks and Recreation Department.

1857: A second above-ground Powder Magazine is erected at the north end of Jefferson Barracks. This stone building currently serves as a museum and is maintained by the St. Louis County Parks and Recreation Department.

1861: Military troops from Jefferson Barracks surround the pro-secessionist Camp Jackson in St. Louis. When the pro-secessionist troops surrender, the Federal Arsenal and its valuable ammunition and weapons in St. Louis are retained by the Union. In the same year, construction of the post's hospital is completed.

1862: Jefferson Barracks falls under the control of the Army Medical Department and becomes the largest most influential Federal medical facility in the United States.

1863: President Abraham Lincoln, by Executive Order, expands the "Old Post Cemetery" south of Jefferson Barracks, and creates the 4th most active National Cemetery in the country.

October 29, 1864: the Union Army executed Six Confederate prisoners at Fort #4 in St. Louis. The executions were in retaliation for the Confederate massacre of Major James Wilson and a six-man patrol, during the Battle of Pilot Knob on October 3, 1864. The bodies of the dead Confederate prisoners were later buried at the Jefferson Barracks National Cemetery, section 20, graves 4605-4610.

1866: Arsenal (Quarantine) Island is purchased by the city of St. Louis for quarantine purposes.

1867: Jefferson Barracks becomes an U.S. Army Engineer Depot.

1868: Mr. Martin Burke is appointed as the second Superintendent of the Jefferson Barracks National Cemetery. Mr. Burke would later unearth the remains of several "unidentified" children whose graves had been obscured by bushes and undergrowth in the Old Post Section of the cemetery.

April 1876: The remains of 470 soldiers buried on Quarantine Island are moved and reinterred at the Jefferson Barracks National Cemetery.

1878: Jefferson Barracks becomes a U.S. Army Calvary Depot.

1892: Construction on several new buildings is started. The old stone buildings are torn down and brick barracks and officers quarters are built in their place. A majority of these buildings were completed in 1900. Many of these buildings are in use today by various Missouri Army and Air National Guard units.

1896: Jefferson Barracks if further "modernized" when streetcar service is extended from St. Louis to the post.

1898: Jefferson Barracks is designated as a "stepping off point" for soldiers taking part in the Spanish-American War.

July 3, 1898: The Spanish battleship *Oquenda* is sunk in Santiago Bay.

1899: A canon from the battleship *Oquenda* is presented to Jefferson Barracks. This highly treasured trophy of the Spanish-American War is on display behind Building 1, overlooking the Mississippi River.

1900: Building 1, presently the post's Headquarters, is constructed.

April 15, 1904: The remains of the officers and soldiers buried at Fort

Bellefountaine are moved and reentered at the Jefferson Barracks National Cemetery. A large granite boulder erected by the St. Louis Chapter of the Daughters of the American Revolution, memorializes these 'Unknown' soldiers.

March 2, 1912: A civilian successfully completes the first parachute jump from an airplane at Jefferson Barracks.

1917-18: Jefferson Barracks comes to life when it serves as the nation's largest induction and demobilization center for military personnel during World War I .

1922: A Veterans Administration Hospital is established at Jefferson Barracks on 170 acres of land south of the cemetery. A Citizens Military Training Camp is established at Jefferson Barracks.

1933: Jefferson Barracks becomes the site of the Civilian Conservation Corps.

1941-45: Jefferson Barracks again heeds the nations call to arms, and serves as an induction and separation center during World War II. The post would later become the largest technical training school for the Army Air Corps. Over 400 German and Italian prisoners of war are housed at Jefferson Barracks. Two German prisoners and Five Italian prisoners died while at Jefferson Barracks, and their bodies were buried at the National Cemetery.

1946: The U.S. military closes Jefferson Barracks. All but 135 acres of the post, what is currently the Jefferson Barracks Missouri Air National Guard Base, is declared surplus by the War Department.

1950: St. Louis County Parks and Recreation Department take over 500 acres of the closed post. Jefferson Barracks park is created.

February 14, 1952: On this date, 123 Army and Navy service men who died while prisoners of the Japanese Imperial Army, were buried at the Jefferson Barracks National Cemetery. On December 14, 1944, these brave American soldiers were brutally massacred by their captors.

1970-98: Various Missouri Army, Air National Guard Units, U.S. Army Reserve Units and U.S. Naval Reserve Units, occupy Jefferson Barracks.

July 11, 1998: 1st Lt. Michael Blassie is reinterred at the National Cemetery. The remains of 1st Lt. Blassie, a pilot who had been shot down over Vietnam in 1972, had been previously entombed with the "Unknowns" in Arlington National Cemetery for fourteen years. 1st Lt. Blassie's remains had been moved to Jefferson Barracks after modern forensic DNA tests positively identified them as being his, on June 30, 1998

November 1998, 1st Lt. David Goodwin is assigned to HHD, 1138th Engineer Battalion, Building 27, as the Battalion Logistics Officer (S4).

October 1999 to Present: 1st Lt. (later promoted to Captain) David Goodwin becomes Detachment Commander, HHD 1138th Engineer Battalion, Building 27.

BIBLIOGRAPHY

Alabama Center for Health Studies ~ Mortality Patterns: Then and Now (1999)
Army National Guard Retention Planner
Bartels, Carolyn ~ The Civil War in Missouri Day By Day 1861 to 1865 (1992)
Bear Facts ~ "Funeral Honor Team Performs 10,000th Service" (article 2001)
Billings, John S. ~ A Report on Barracks and Hospitals, with descriptions of Military Posts (1870)
Blue & Gray Magazine ~ Guide To haunted Places Of The Civil War (1996)
Bowers, Michael, eds. ~ North American Fighting Uniforms an Illustrated History Since 1756 (1994)
Brouwer, Rene ~ The First World War 1914-1918 (Internet Website 2001)
Burnett, Betty ~ St. Louis at War (1987)
Conard, Howard, edu.~ Encyclopedia Of The History of Missouri: A Compendium of History and Biography for Ready Reference, Volume III (1901)
Confederate POW's and Prisons in St. Louis (Internet Website)
Courtaway, Robbi ~ Spirits of Saint Louis (1999)
Davis, William C. ~ The Fighting Men Of The Civil War (1999)
Descendants of Mexican War Veterans ~ The U.S. Mexican War 1846-1848 (Internet Website 1996-2001)
Evans, Hilary and Patrick Huyghe ~ The Field Guide to Ghosts and Other Apparitions (2000)
Faherty, Willaim Barnaby ~ St. Louis "A Concise History" (1989)
Fifield, Barringer with Keith Recker ~ Seeing St. Louis (1991)
Figg, Laurann and Jane Farrell-Beck ~ Amputation in the Civil War: Physical and Social Dimensions (Journal of the History of Medicine and Applied Sciences 1993)
Fort Monroe's Casemate Museum ~ Fort Monroe History (Internet Website 2000)
Fort Washita History (Internet Website)
Fusco, Tony ~ A Pictorial History of Jefferson Barracks (1969)
Fusco, Tony ~ Historic Jefferson Barracks: A Collection of Articles from the Naborhood Link News, (09-07-1966 to 08-31-1967)
Fusco, Tony ~ The Story of The Jefferson Barracks National Cemetery (1967)
Givens, Douglas R. ~ Jefferson Barracks Historical Database of Published Records (1993)
Grave of Elizabeth Lash (Internet Website)
Griffith, Paddy ~ Battle In The Civil War (1986)
Guiley, Rosemary Ellen ~ Atlas of The Mysterious In North America (1995)

Guiley, Rosemary Ellen ~ The Encyclopedia Of Ghosts And Spirits (1992)
Hamilton, Alice S., Dennis Naglich and Joseph M. Nixson ~ Report of Phase I Cultural Resource Survey of Jefferson Barracks, Site 23SL656, Air and Army National Guard Facility Southern St. Louis County, Missouri, Research Report #91 (February 1989)
Hanley, George ~ District Buries Unexploded Ordnance (Internet Website 2000)
Hart, Herbert M. ~ Pioneer Forts Of The West (1967)
Hauck, Denis William ~ Haunted Places The National Directory (1994/ 1996)
History Of Missouri (1888/ 1992)
Holzer, Hans ~ Travel Guide To Haunted Houses (1998)
Index Of The Civil War In Missouri, Links and Resources (Internet Website)
Jaegers, Bevy with Jaegers ~ Ghost Hunting (1988)
Jefferson Barracks Park (Pamphlet)
Lethbridge, T.C. ~ Ghost and Ghoul (1961)
Love- Bigony, Mary ~ In Spirit (Internet Website 1998)
McNilty, Elizabeth ~ St. Louis Then and Now (2000)
Military.com ~ 1st Lt. Michael Blassie (Internet Website 2001)
Milligan, Debi ~ Aunt Jane, Where Are you? (Story, Internet Website)
Missouri Air National Guard ~ Historical Pamphlet
Missouri's Fields of Honor (Internet Website)
National Park Service ~ Fort Pulaski National Monument (Internet Website 2001)
Pitcock, Cynthia De Haven ~ William Beaumont, M.D. and Malpractice: The Mary Dugan Case, 1844 (Journal of the History of Medicine and Applied Sciences 1992)
Pratt, Fletcher ~ Civil War in Pictures (1955)
Rush, Loretta G. ~ Whispering Stones: Historical Account of Fort Washita (Internet Website)
Schuermann, Art ~ Chronological History Of Jefferson Barracks (Pamphlet)
Sperry, T.J. and Harry C. Myers ~ A History of Fort Union (Internet Website)
South County Chamber of Commerce ~ Chronological Historical Facts (Internet Website 2000)
St. Louis Parks and Recreation ~ Jefferson Barracks (Internet Website)
Swofford, Daniel ~ America at War "American Military History: Revolutionary War to World War II (Internet Website 1991)
Taylor, Troy ~ Beyond The Grave (2001)
Taylor, Troy ~ Haunted Illinois (1999)
Taylor, Troy ~ The Phantom Funeral of Fort De Chartres (Internet Website 2000)
Taylor, Troy ~ Spirits of the Civil War (1999)
Taylor, Troy ~ The Ghost Hunters Guidebook (2001)

Taylor, Troy ~ The Ghost Hunters Handbook (1997)
Taylor, Troy ~ The Ghosts Of Fort Washita (Internet Website 1998)
Texas Parks and Wildlife ~ Fort Mckavett State Historical Park (Internet Website)
The Center For Archaeological Studies, University of South Alabama ~ Fort De Chartres III, Prairie Du Rocher, Illinois (Internet Website 2001)
The Company of Military Historians ~ Military Uniforms In America Long Endure: The Civil War Period 1852 - 1867 (1982)
The Hauntings of Fort Monroe, Virginia (Internet Website 2001)
The Spanish American War Centennial Website ~ (Internet Website 1996-2001)
Time-Life ~ History Of The Civil War (1990)
Toney, B. Keith ~ Battle Field Ghosts (1997)
University of Missouri-St. Louis Museum Studies Program ~ Jefferson Barracks: A Celebration of the Citizen Soldier (2001)
U.S. Army in Action - The Rock of the Marne (Historical Information Poster)
U.S. Department of Veterans Affairs (Internet Website)
Welcome To Jefferson Barracks National Cemetery ~ Pamphlet, BSA Troop 905
Winter, William C. ~ The Civil War in St. Louis (1995)

Personal Interviews and Correspondence

Note from the Publisher: Although Whitechapel Productions Press, Troy Taylor, and all affiliated with this book have carefully researched all sources to insure the accuracy of the information contained in this book, we assume no responsibility for errors, inaccuracies or omissions.

ACKNOWLEDGEMENTS

When I first started researching and writing this book, I thought that it would be a solitary journey of personal discovery. Boy was I wrong! I quickly learned that it takes more than one person to write a book. If anything, this book has helped me realize that it takes many talented friends and fellow professionals, working behind the scenes, to ensure that any literary endeavor is a success.

I am personally indebted to all of the soldiers and civilians who took time out of their busy schedules to share their stories with me. I would like to especially recognize Sergeant Duane Fly, Senior Master Sergeant Art Schuermann, Carol Wheeler, Chief Master Sergeant Eugene Anacker (Retired), and Technical Sergeant Tony Fusco (Retired) for their contributions to the historical research required for this book.

In addition to those already mentioned, I am grateful to Staff Sergeant Glenn McFarland, Master Sergeant Jerry Faust, Master Sergeant John Sonntag, Richard Platz, and Jim and Linda Luehrs for all of their help in making this book a reality.

A special note of thanks goes to Troy Taylor. Troy has been my mentor on this project from the very beginning. His support and down to earth advice have been invaluable to me throughout each phase of this pilgrimage.

Lastly, I want to thank my wife Lisa and my stepson Todd. Without their patience, and encouragement, this book would not have been possible.

This book is dedicated to all of the men and women who have ever served at Jefferson Barracks and to my "Sweet Baby Girl" Tessa, who was born on 08-11-2001. May her eyes be forever open to the boundless wonders of our world.

ABOUT THE AUTHOR

David Goodwin is a Sergeant and Lead Investigator for the Protective Services Department at the Washington University School of Medicine, and a commissioned Reserve Deputy with the Warren County Sheriff's Department. He has a Bachelors degree in law enforcement from Northern Michigan University (NMU) and has worked in the law enforcement and campus security field for over eight years.

Dave enlisted in the Michigan Army National Guard in 1986. He was commissioned as a 2nd Lieutenant in 1992 after completing the Reserve Officer Training Corps (ROTC) program at NMU and currently holds the rank of Captain. Dave is the Commander of the Headquarters Detachment, 1138th Engineer Battalion, stationed at Jefferson Barracks.

Dave has actively investigated numerous haunted locations for the last ten years. He has been an active member of the American Ghost Society (AGS) for over four years and currently serves as one of the organization's St. Louis Area Representatives. Dave has also been a member of the Ghost Research Society (GRS) for over eight years and currently serves as one of the organizations Missouri State Coordinators.

On October 19, 1994, Dave married Lisa Wever. Dave, Lisa and their children currently live in Black Jack, Missouri.

ABOUT WHITECHAPEL PRODUCTIONS PRESS

Whitechapel Productions Press is a small press publisher, specializing in books about ghosts and hauntings. Since 1993, the company has been one of America's leading publishers of supernatural books. Located in Alton, Illinois, they also produce the "Ghosts of the Prairie" internet web page.

In addition to publishing books on history and hauntings, they also host and distribute the Haunted America Catalog, which features over 500 different books about ghosts and hauntings from authors all over the United States. A complete selection of these books can be browsed in person at the "History & Hauntings Book Co." Store in Alton.

Visit Whitechapel Productions Press on the internet and browse through our selection of over ghostly titles, plus information on ghosts and hauntings; haunted history; spirit photographs; information on ghost hunting and much more. Visit the internet web page at:

www.prairieghosts.com

Or visit the Haunted Book Co. in Person at:

515 East Third Street
Alton, Illinois t2002
(618)-456-1086

For More on Haunted St. Louis, see Troy Taylor's Book -

Haunted St. Louis
History & Hauntings Along the Mississippi

CPSIA information can be obtained at www.ICGtesting.com
Printed in the USA
BVOW09s1349151015

422420BV00005B/59/P